IN THE NAME OF THE LORD

IN THE NAME OF THE LORD

A NUN'S TELL-ALL

SISTER LUCY KALAPURA

TRANSLATED FROM THE MALAYALAM BY
NANDAKUMAR K.
CO-WINNER OF THE JCB PRIZE FOR LITERATURE

HarperCollins *Publishers* India

First published in Malayalam as *Karthavinte Naamathil* by DC Books in 2019

First published in India in English by HarperCollins *Publishers* 2022
4th Floor, Tower A, Building No. 10, Phase II, DLF Cyber City,
Gurugram, Haryana – 122002
www.harpercollins.co.in

By arrangement with DC Books

2 4 6 8 10 9 7 5 3 1

Copyright © Sister Lucy Kalapura 2019, 2022
Translation copyright © Nandakumar K. 2022

P-ISBN: 978-93-5489-198-4
E-ISBN: 978-93-5489-085-7

The views and opinions expressed in this book are the author's own and the facts are as reported by her, and the publishers are not in any way liable for the same.

Sister Lucy Kalapura asserts the moral right
to be identified as the author of this work.

For sale in the Indian subcontinent only

All rights reserved. No part of this publication may be reproduced, stored in a retrieval system, or transmitted, in any form or by any means, electronic, mechanical, photocopying, recording or otherwise, without the prior permission of the publishers.

Typeset in 11/15 Minion Pro at
Manipal Technologies Limited, Manipal

Printed and bound at
Thomson Press (India) Ltd

This book is produced from independently certified FSC® paper
to ensure responsible forest management.

Dedicated to my loving father, Scaria, and my mother, Rosa, who have made me what I am today
—Sister Lucy Kalapura

Dedicated to my friend Rajesh, who has egged me on in whatever I choose to do.
—Nandakumar K.

Translator's Note

When HarperCollins offered me *Karthavinte Naamathil* by Sister Lucy Kalapura, published in Malayalam by DC Books, for translation, I had not read the book yet.

When I took it up, it was, therefore, a leap of faith, in a manner of speaking.

Sister Lucy is not the first one to fall foul of the Catholic Church. She will not be the last either.

But there are stories that must be told and must be heard. Hers is one of them. I was curious to know what makes her so daring that she could stand up to the might of the Church, which is often not, despite the much-touted Christian spirit, very forgiving to whoever crosses it.

It is not for me to cast the first stone, but the reader will discover that frivolous charges were brought on to throw Sister Lucy out of the congregation when others who have mortally sinned—as opposed to her venial sins, if at that—still continue to be people of the cloth and hold responsible positions.

Here was an example of power potent enough to crush being used with premeditation and purpose, expecting there would be no resistance and no push-back. Often, power is wielded only with this expectation: that the victim will be too soft to resist, or their best can still be worsted.

What the Church did not reckon with was the feistiness of Sister Lucy and her staying power. Such feistiness must come from deep faith and the belief that one has right on one's side—it is not blind rashness or hubris. For instance, some time after this book was written, when she went to the court against her expulsion, she had to argue her case all by herself as no lawyer, for understandable reasons considering whom they would be arguing against, was ready to take up her case. It certainly could not have been on pecuniary considerations.

Her appeals to the Vatican were turned down. There was not a remote chance that—despite the pontiff publicly admitting that mortal sin does take place in churches, monasteries and convents—her appeal would be upheld, though what set off the events was her joining the protest against Bishop Franco Mulakkal of Jalandhar after he was accused of raping a nun.

Sister Lucy too would have known that. So, it is remarkable that she decided to stick to her guns and did not back down. The pressure brought to bear on her must have been immense, enough to crack a lesser human being. This story would not have been written if she were made of less stern stuff.

However, we are getting ahead of ourselves. This book tells her story till her expulsion from her congregation and the events leading up to it.

Different styles are used to narrate stories. The person who had helped Sister Lucy write the book in Malayalam seems to have been a great believer in brevity. If the reader perceives gaps in the story and yearns for the details, it can be ascribed to this belief in brevity. Since this is a translation, it was decided by the publisher and myself that the book should stick to the original.

I would like to thank Dr Fathima E.V. for recommending me to HarperCollins. My gratitude to my friend and mentor, a Catholic himself, who in true Christian spirit painstakingly went through the manuscript, corrected my errors, explained the sacraments and the hierarchy of the Church to a non-Christian, and polished the text. My gratitude also to Siddhesh Inamdar of HarperCollins for his constant guidance and encouragement. I am also beholden to Suchismita Ukil for her attention to detail, painstaking interventions in the copy, and leaving nothing unchallenged.

Nandakumar K.
March 2022

Preface

Like any ordinary girl, I passed through the physical and psychological changes that occur during the natural progression from childhood, through adolescence, to adulthood. I didn't show any extraordinary life skills during my student days. The idea of becoming a nun was my reaction to the prospect of living as a social animal. I was born into a family imbued with the spirit of Christianity. My comfortable life and upbringing only served to nurture and fortify the spirituality in me.

The Christian faith underpinned the ethos of the settlers in the remote hillside village of Karikkottakary in Kannur district. Kannur used to be the northern-most district of Kerala till Kasaragod was hived off in 1984 and became the border district between Kerala and Karnataka. It is possible that the faith of the settlers was part of their survival tactics and strategies. My family residence was on the banks of the Vempuzha river that originates in the village of Ayyankunnu in Kannur and flows into the Bavali river. Till I became an adolescent, I wasn't even aware there was a world beyond the bank of this river and, in any case, beyond what the eyes could see.

I had no knowledge of how life went on in places such as Kottukappara, Edoor, Mundayamparamba, Parakkappara and Edappuzha that lay around us. The majority of the settlers in these localities were people from lower-caste groups who had converted to Christianity. They were looked down upon and often humiliated by the rich, landed gentry among the Christians, whose forebears were formerly higher-caste Hindus. I came to know only later that their lives were transformed by the advent of the Reverend Father Joseph Taffarel and his evangelism.

I was surrounded by a big family consisting of ten siblings and my parents. My outside world comprised the church, its priest and catechism classes. These environs were instrumental in infusing convents, nuns and the gospel into my mind.

My untroubled, carefree childhood culminated in the resolution to take my vows as a Bride of Christ, as nuns were described among the faithful. It was not a call of God that I had answered; my resolution was not born out of the blue. For a long time, I had waited for the summons from Christ. Perhaps a puerile stubbornness led me to become a nun. I had channelled the spring of natural energy and verve for life that surges during adolescence and youth into Christian spirituality. An inscrutable stream of consciousness led me to be a maid of God. The demarcation between truth and falsehood was imperceptible as far as I was concerned.

I spent almost a lifetime in search of the essence of the hollow pronouncements that I heard around me. Only much later would I come to realize that what was being declaimed and propagandized was complete fiction. In what was reminiscent of ovine submissiveness, Christ's brides, powerless to resist, were herded down a nefariously built path without even a glance backwards. It was my conviction that I couldn't go forward in that sheeplike manner, and that led me to a new and different destiny and path.

My hopes were nurtured and grew in the bright and airy cloisters of the convent. Today, in convents, I see a congregation of independent individuals with good, hard common sense, ready to do social service. I also believe it is time to reform the priest-dominant culture in the Christian world and rewrite its rules. I am also certain that a gospel community that reflects the fundamental tenets of Christian asceticism—poverty, obedience and chastity—will also emerge.

I believe in the power and mercy of Jesus Christ. I hold on to no regrets about the unconditional love I have for him. But the muted cries of my unfortunate sisters, whose lives are crushed within the forbidding walls of convents, hurt my ears. I wish this testament will become a guiding light to those who are cursed to writhe under the trampling feet of dominant paternalism and authoritarian priesthood.

With the good Lord as my witness, I testify that all that I have said here is the truth. This is not merely my life story; it is that of all my sisters who have been dragooned into taking the vows. I believe that I am fulfilling the mission Jesus Christ has given me. In my life's journey, I have neither friends nor enemies. I accept this dualism with the same ready forbearance. In my narrative, I have taken names for veracity and not to make any personal remarks about those named. The miserable lives that the nuns are forced to live are the result of a rotten system. The words and phrases of the book are a testament to one's liberation from the dungeons of ignorance and bondage. Personal vilification is not my purpose. I am merely narrating my life without fear or favour.

Sister Lucy Kalapura

Chapter One

Only some time remained until the momentous hour. I was contented and untroubled. My father, uncle, mother, siblings—none could pierce my equanimity. As I remained smiling, it didn't even occur to me that I was being observed by others in that well-populated house of ours. My mind and heart were somewhere beyond all that, in an unknown space. I was intrepid. I was determined. My mind was made up irrevocably. It was not a wanton desire born in a fickle moment. True, it wasn't a desire that pleased anyone in our big family. But none of this was going to persuade me to change my decision.

In a way, this Lucy was leaving home for good.

Let me begin with the incidents of the previous day. I was humming happily. Preparations for my upcoming journey were being made almost as if reflexively. The day passed quickly and it was evening soon. While ironing my clothes, my humming turned into loud singing. Everyone around was staring at me; I was oblivious to their quizzical looks.

I have decided to follow Jesus;
No turning back, no turning back.
The world behind me, the cross before me;
No turning back, no turning back.
Though none go with me, still I will follow;
No turning back, no turning back.
My cross I'll carry, till I see Jesus;
No turning back, no turning back.
Will you decide now to follow Jesus?
No turning back, no turning back.

An intense desire to get there was impelling me. I stacked my clothes neatly in the suitcase. Though everyone around me was grieving, they didn't let it show. They walked about with bowed heads, hiding the sadness on their faces and avoiding eye contact with one another. Chachan, as I called my father, sat in his usual chair, gloomily observing everything, even though his head stayed bowed. My mother, busy in the kitchen, stuck her head out now and then to check on me. She was one of the bravest women I have met in my life. I have never seen her cry. At dinner, everyone was silent. I had finished packing; I ate my dinner in silence and went to my bedroom. I did not realize then that something out of the ordinary was going to happen. I fell asleep, calm as ever.

After I woke early in the morning and got ready for my journey, I hugged my mother and kissed her on the forehead. That hug energized me. I felt more powerful than before.

No one had stood in the way of my desire to become a nun. When I first broached the subject with my father, his initial response had been to deny me permission. There was a reason for this; he and Kunjaanjaa (my eldest brother) were aware of the rivalries and hostilities among nuns. One of my older sisters had joined the convent before me. The entire family had opposed her decision.

Nevertheless, she wouldn't be dissuaded. She fought and left my family with no other option but to give her the approval she wanted.

The experience with my sister was in their minds when I decided to don the habit. This is why, even though they expressed their displeasure, no one put up any serious resistance. After bidding everyone goodbye, I left home with unfaltering steps. Chachan was with me in the car. My memories kept validating my decision. Having lived in relative comfort, I had no misgivings about why I had made that decision about my future.

Chapter Two

THE KALAPURAKKALS WERE ONE OF THE WEALTHY FAMILIES IN Karikkottakary village. My grandfather and his family had moved from Kuravilangad in Kottayam in 1940 and had settled here. Since they had come with money, they bought land in Karikkottakary—almost fifty acres. They tilled the virgin land and turned it into farmland. Around the same period, many others had migrated from south Kerala or Thiruvithamkoor, as the region was known, and settled here. The majority of them were Christians. Along with food crops, they also planted rubber and pepper.

The bulk of the migration had taken place due to a famine. These migrants bought land using money from the sale of land in their native places and supplemented by their savings. As there were large tracts of untenanted fertile lands, some became squatters. My grandfather had one more son apart from my father. We children used to call him Pappan. He and my father had five sisters.

My grandfather's lifestyle was typical of people in the region. He was liked by the village folk and respected by everyone. I remember he was a dapper gentleman; he was in his seventies then. Pleasant-faced and fair-complexioned, he had a determined look on his face. His name was Scaria. As was my father's and Kunjaanjaa's. My grandfather had an imperious bearing. Our house was always noisy and loud, but in his presence it remained quiet.

Inside the house, he used to wear only a loincloth and over it a *torthu*, a loosely woven towel. However, when he left the house, he would wear only starched, spotless, white clothes. Water used to be kept ready in a *kindi,* a spouted, gold-coloured alloy water pot, for him to wash his hands before and after meals. As he used to chew *paan*, a spittoon would always be found in his vicinity. There was a seat in the house that he had reserved for his use. He was a disciplined and self-contained man, with a schedule for everything—waking up, dressing, eating, praying. For him, everything had a place and a time—something that I have tried to emulate in my life too.

He used to wind the clock in the prayer room, where he and my grandmother used to sleep. Evening prayers used to be at 7.30 p.m. sharp. After I grew up, I used to be summoned for prayers on religious days. His ways and manners were distinct and inimitable. He owned a bullock cart, which in those days was our primary vehicle. It was used to carry our farm produce to the market and fetch groceries and other essentials for the household on the way back.

Kalapurakkal Scaria was a patriarch. He was fit and healthy. He oversaw everything. His hallmark was the punctuality with which he followed his daily routine. I can still see him in my mind's eye, clothed in his sparkling white shirt and *mundu* as he set off for the market. He was so punctual that there were neighbours who timed their own daily activities with his time of leaving the house. He taught us, his grandchildren, to tell the time by looking at the strength of the daylight and the length of the shadows. Possibly it was this kind of grounding in precision that led me to become a teacher of mathematics. Later, I often used cos, sin and tan to counter my grandfather's native proficiency in arithmetic.

He had set timings for going to the market, exchanging pleasantries and returning home. The sandals he used to wear would be washed and left to dry, leaning against the wall at a precise spot every day. On his return, he would hang the clothes on a wooden hanger he had made himself. His clothes would have no wrinkles and creases. A piece of cloth was set aside by him to be used exclusively to dry his feet after washing them. And even that piece of cloth had a specific place.

He liked his food prepared in different styles. He would buy fish and other provisions from the market on specific days. Some of this fish he would buy only for himself. As soon as he reached home, he would summon my mother and hand it over. It would be cooked and kept in a special compartment of the rice chest in the dining room. I have seen my mother make special efforts to prepare the dish and serve him.

I have seen him ill only once. That was on his deathbed. I bathed him twice during those days.

A sight I was fond of was sugar being filled into narrow-mouthed tall crocks; we used to call them *cheena bharani*. It was done meticulously, without a single grain of sugar being spilled. I never missed an opportunity to watch this chore being performed; I would find time for it even when preoccupied with something else.

When the property was divided, the main house went to Pappan. My grandfather was staying in that house with Pappan, but it was not in his destiny to continue to do so for an extended period of time. The division of the property happened before I was born. My parents moved to their new residence with their four young children. Since we had large tracts of land, we employed a large number of workers too. My mother had to struggle to cook for all of them and take care of her own brood. My grandmother had offered to come along, but my mother did not accept the offer in order to spare her the inconvenience of having to live in the new place.

One day, after they had moved, my mother thought she saw a cot making its way on its own towards our new house. Only when it got closer did she realize that it was grandfather bearing the cot he slept on in the main house. He brought over grandmother's cot also the same day. Within a couple of days, they moved to our house, lock, stock and barrel.

Pappan and his family could not adjust to the quirky traits of my grandfather as much as my mother had been able to. My grandfather had a toilet built for himself near the river, which was a novelty and source of amazement for the denizens of our village. It was built according to his own design. He had rigid ideas about cleaning its environs. The toilet was not made of masonry, and it was not fully built up. Though the rare passers-by could see him communing with nature, he didn't exactly mind it. They also didn't mind, for that matter.

He was a devout Christian though not overly religious. Evening prayers were never given a miss. During the church festival, he gave all his grandchildren money to drop in the collection box. The eleven of us used to stand in a queue to receive the handouts. I always thought it was a pretty sight, the way he used to take the money out of the black wallet kept in his waistband.

*

As faithful believers, we used to wait with great anticipation for the parish festival every year. We children were drawn by the multi-coloured ribbons, balloons and toys at the church grounds. Our eyes and hearts were set on the colourful trinkets and baubles that filled the temporary stalls. I always used up the money given by grandfather to buy such stuff. I wasn't keen to attend the mass on the day of the festival.

Kunjaanjaa used to say it was better to distribute the money among the beggars on the way than drop it in the offerings box. His argument was that God would be happier with compassion towards others. Piety is what is perceived by others. That must be one of the first instances when I started to feel that God is present where there is truth and love. God was born as a man for those who couldn't accept and experience a formless God. I realized even as a child that my concept of God was different from that of other children.

In our noisy, bustling household, Chachan was my role model. I have not seen him engaged in manual work. Tall and statuesque, he was popular among all the people of our village. He was addressed as Kunjettan or little big brother by everyone. I can only remember him with admiration.

Those days our parish had five hundred families; now, there are more than two thousand. He was close to everyone and had cordial relations with all. He used to be arbitrator and mediator for all disputes in the village. Before they approached the vicar, the people would meet Chachan and try to resolve their disputes. Though he didn't belong to any political party nor was a leader, he would be requested to intervene in all matters. He would try his utmost to find solutions for people's poverty and privations. He even used to borrow money and help people in need.

I recall that even in difficult circumstances, Chachan had given our maid, Eliyamma *chechi*, money to dig a well near her house. The doctors had diagnosed that he had a leaking valve in his heart. So he was not allowed by my mother and others to exert himself physically. Yet, while it was being dug, I heard that he even descended into the well to help, ignoring the strong objections of those present.

We had five or six household workers. Narayanan *atten* and his family used to stay on our land and do the chores.

Chachan used to give equal importance to our family matters. His weak heart kept him away from agriculture. Kunjaanjaa wasn't interested in farming either. Only my second brother among us eleven children was involved in our traditional occupation of farming.

Chachan had a major heart surgery in his early fifties. He was so progressive, caring and prudent that before going to the hospital he summoned his two eldest sons and partitioned his estate equitably so that those with less education got a bigger share. Except for my two brothers, he did not let anyone in on this; even my mother wasn't informed. He had thought that he might not survive the surgery and was thinking of everyone's welfare even while contemplating that he may not make it.

My father was punctilious in keeping accounts. He was invited to join the school that had been built adjacent to the church. He was the leader of the volunteer parishioners who constructed the thatched school building. Considering the times, he had received a decent education—he had studied up to Class 7—and had been offered a job as a teacher. However, he demurred. He felt a job would cramp his style and be a hindrance to his public life.

My mother, Rosa, was always a brave heroine for me. She also had a basic education, the first in her family to get one. When she had completed her Class 5 exams, her family shifted to a different place and that brought an end to her formal education as there were no schools in the new area. She made and controlled the budget of the household. Chachan used to give my mother the day's earnings after selling the produce. When he needed to borrow money from others, he used to do so only after seeking my mother's concurrence.

Though we were a large family, we didn't compete with one another or try to outdo one another. We sat together for supper. Chachan used to sit at the small dining table. We children would take our plates and park ourselves wherever we could find space. Dinnertime was when matters of import were presented. We never pointed fingers; we never discussed the shortcomings or errors of anyone. This was banned by Chachan and my mother.

Chapter Three

I STARTED MY SCHOOLING IN ST. THOMAS SCHOOL, KARIKKOTTAKARY. I was a very ordinary girl with no remarkable talent. However, I was a diligent student. We had all learnt the Malayalam alphabet from our mother before we started school. Even in the midst of her busy schedule, she had found time to teach her children at least the rudiments of language. I had a happy, contented childhood. We brothers and sisters used to walk to school together. Our walk to and from school was full of mirth and good cheer, and we walked at a leisurely pace, making small talk with birds and the waters of the Payassini river, and caressing every blade of grass on the way.

Chachan denied us nothing. New clothes would be made before the school reopened every year. Chachan and mother had set a schedule for all these preparations. I have good memories of my first teacher—my mother; in those fond memories, she always appears in her white *chatta*, a kind of loose blouse and *mundu*, a cloth draped like a sarong and worn with a fantail at the back.

One of my earliest memories—in one of my primary classes—is of a girl drenched to the skin. She was wailing and sobbing. Water was dripping down her dress. Her hair was wet; tears mingled with the water flowing down her cheeks. I couldn't control my own sadness. I felt a cloudburst of compassion; I rushed to her side. Without taking off her dress, I tried to wring the water out as much as I could. I wiped her face with my hands and seated her next to me. She was from a poor family who couldn't afford an umbrella. Before our classes were over and we left for home, I gave her my new umbrella. I saw the sparkle of happiness in her eyes. Chachan was my guru in such matters too. I realized that the bliss that one experiences while showing mercy to a fellow being would take one closer to God.

When I got home, Chachan asked me about my umbrella. I had no hesitation in telling him the truth. Not only did he not scold me, he even praised me. By nature, I was drawn to people facing difficulties and sorrows. I seem to have some affinity for the poor. This was positively encouraged at home. I was devoid of selfishness. My good marks made me the pet of my teachers, who were all nuns. I wanted to spread the fragrance of God's goodness. This could be the reason for my fascination with the cloister, even at the young age of ten or twelve years.

None of us attended mass on any day other than Sunday. During the service and sermon, a pall of disinterest, and of detachment, used to descend over me. My only wish was to do good to others. My heart pined for the sight of happiness in others' eyes. The only path I could see in front of me was to become a Bride of Jesus Christ. However, this desire didn't stay with me for long. By the time I was in high school, convents, nuns and mother superiors had been replaced in my heart by the concept of social service.

An old woman lived in one corner of the church land, in a hut built for her by the church authorities near an open ground. During our lunch hour, along with a few friends, I used to go to her place. We would sweep the house and its environs for her. At home, my mother never forced any of us to do household chores. Yet, I was never unwilling to clean that old woman's place. My heart yearned to spend more time with her. I used to bring her rice and coconut from home. I was certain that my love for Jesus Christ was being manifested through the kindness shown to the old woman. At that time, I wasn't even aware that the Gospel according to Matthew was relevant in my case.

> *For I was hungry and you gave me something to eat, I was thirsty and you gave me something to drink, I was a stranger and you invited me in, I needed clothes and you clothed me, I was sick and you looked after me, I was in prison and you came to visit me.*
>
> Matthew 25:35–39

Until I finished Class 10, my mind was stuck on social service. The cloister was not on my mind, nor did any career appeal to me. I found myself uninterested in everything; nothing captured my imagination. Teaching and medicine held no attraction. I thought poorly of engineering and the civil services. Although English, Hindi and mathematics were my favourite subjects in school, my only aim was to become a dedicated social worker.

My school life passed smoothly. As far I remember, I missed class only one day—to attend my nephew's baptism. The next day, my class teacher asked for my leave application. I wasn't aware that such a system existed. When I expressed my inability to produce one, he got angry. He insisted that the leave letter had to be produced that instant. I was allowed to enter the class only after I got one written by my brother, who was running a parallel college—as non-regular colleges were known in Kerala—near my school, and submitted it. I have still not been able to fathom that teacher's animosity towards me.

During my schooldays, I didn't have close friends. I used to keep everyone at a distance. I was not attracted to the things that fascinated other girls of my age. A steadfast, unbending will was a unique trait in me. I also had a penchant for taking decisions and carrying them out scrupulously.

My parents were an ideal couple in my view. As a family, we were close-knit; we didn't have much to do with the outside world. Our world was our family and the house we lived in. As the seventh-born among eleven children, I respected and loved my elder brothers from a distance. By the time we younger ones were studying in the primary sections, the elder ones had already passed out of college. This meant that there was distance in our relationship. However, we all shared a special fondness for Kunjaanjaa.

We used to have a radio when it was not yet common or easily accessible. Though my grandfather was its rightful owner, we used to listen to the All India Radio news, film songs and other entertainment programmes on it. During Kunjaanjaa's student days in Devagiri College, he once brought a tape recorder home. That was a source of wonderment for us. I remember all of us going to bed very late on that moonlit night. We sang songs or made speeches, which were recorded and played back to us. We recorded a hilarious feature on our grandfather, mimicking the radio news, and played it to him. It was one of the rare occasions when he didn't have a quick response.

*

My heart, set upon social service as it was, had no place for priests and vicars. I was haunted by something that I discovered when I was in secondary school. I noticed that the more buxom girls in my class used to be called to visit the vicar's room regularly. Curiosity got the better of me. I had noticed that after they entered, the doors of the room would be shut. I shared my observation with a few friends and we wondered how to find out what was happening. On one such occasion, helped by some of them, I clambered up and looked through the ventilator pane above the window. I was shocked to see the vicar fondling and caressing the girl. Completely flustered, I leapt down and ran away without saying anything to my friends.

I was unable to contain the emotions that the scene had caused in me. Bewildered, I decided to confide in my mother as soon as I reached home. To my surprise, my mother advised me not to tell this to anyone else and to forget about it. I obeyed her. It was much later that I came to know that my elder sisters also had been through similar experiences and my mother's advice to them had been the same.

I passed my Class 10 examinations with high distinction. It was during my quest for a vocation that would allow me to do social service all the time that the prospect of a monastic life flashed before me. Thoughts about joining the convent started to rise again in my mind. With each passing moment, they gained strength. Failure was not a habit with me. Decisions started to form. They evolved and matured in time.

I had the same approach when it came to convincing my parents to let me go. The good that one does for others should not become servility. I believe that so must love be, too. We must free those whom we love. There was no self-interest in any of the kind deeds. And so I knew that it was only right to expect them to set me free.

Once I had decided to become a nun, the first persons I confided in were the nuns of Karikkottakary convent. At that point, I was besotted with Jesus Christ—he was the owner of my mind and body. The nuns were elated. They were pleased that they had managed to draw a member of the well-to-do and reputable Kalapurakkal family to their fold. Enthused, the same night at dinnertime I made my declaration to the entire family. My voice was firm. Chachan tried to dissuade me at first; my mother didn't say much.

*

I decided to stay at the convent and do my pre-degree course from the nearby Nirmalagiri College, Koothuparamba. Chachan accompanied me to the college when I went to get admission. By then, the convent's management was aware of my decision. At the college, Chachan paid the tuition and hostel fees for my stay in the convent and accompanied me to its gate. His eyes told me to be brave.

I became an inmate there. Except for Mary Kappil and myself, everyone else was a nun.

I took to praying in the chapel when I began college. Some teachers from my college were also residents of the convent. They cared for me and had faith in me. One day a beggar came to the convent, but Mother Superior refused to give alms. Just then, the words of the hymn '*God keeps a record of every help rendered to fellow humans*' sprang to my lips. It started with me humming but soon the whole song was spilling out of my mouth. Mother Superior's testy response was, 'Lucy, go fetch the money for the alms from your home then.'

I was invariably caught in the act during my mischievous antics. Once I felt like having some of the *copra* (desiccated coconut) left to dry on the convent roof. There was no one there at the time. When I picked up a piece and turned around, I found myself staring straight at Mother Superior's face. My honesty, too, resulted in my incurring the displeasure of many.

I returned home during the occasional holidays. In the meantime, a few unbecoming incidents had taken place in the convent. Mutual respect between the nuns was a rare commodity there. They fought; they blamed one another; they stopped talking to one another. They grew envious of one another and bore grudges. This discord and unpleasantness around disturbed me. But the passion for Jesus Christ that was blazing inside me continued unabated. All the answers converged on proximity to God.

The lava of adolescent urges was sloshing about inside me and adding to my disquiet, but the impulses died very soon. My younger self had become one with Jesus Christ. I felt I should only regard him, emulate him, live like him and ignore everyone else. I was resolute in my decision to follow the footsteps of Jesus Christ.

After completing my pre-degree course, I returned home. I was still determined to don the habit. I had no other conception of what to do with myself. I unhesitatingly confessed to the nuns that I had decided to follow Jesus Christ. To me, that was the sole path to dedicate my life in the service of others. The call of God doesn't happen in an instant; it comes from deep inside one's life. In essence, it is life itself. The call of God is the bidding from one's innate goodness and benevolence.

I started my formation at Thamarassery Diocese's Franciscan Clarist Convent at Koodathai, along with fourteen other sisters. We didn't have any rigorous tasks to do. I participated happily in cleaning the chapel, setting up flower arrangements and Bible studies. I was an expert in making flower baskets; my baskets would be kept at the tabernacle for the Blessed Sacrament. On many occasions, I was complimented for their comeliness. I was chosen to lead our group of fourteen. I used to make jokes whenever errors crept in during the service due to mistakes made by the students of a nearby seminary. Likewise, they also would never let go of an opportunity to mock us. This also led to minor tiffs between the two groups.

Life was fun with dance and play despite the formation training we had to undergo and duties we had to fulfil. Those were trouble-free days. Playing cards was one of the pastimes of the nuns; I, however, had no interest in it. The others tried to persuade me to play, and once, after I refused and they continued to play, the mistress chanced upon them and berated and chased them away.

My smiling face was a reflection of my ingenuousness. As I loved everyone and had a sense of humour, I had no reservations against laughing out loud. I also loved to sleep.

After I completed the initial period of aspirancy, for the next stage of postulancy in my formation, I was sent to the St. Francis Convent, run by the Franciscan Clarist Congregation (FCC), in Dwaraka, Mananthavady.

Chapter Four

MONASTICISM AND PRIESTHOOD ARE NOT PARAMOUNT IN NOR DO they define Christianity. The family is God's voice. Life as a sacrifice starts from the day of one's marriage and it remains replete with sacrifices. The oblation and offertory also start from that point. Giving birth to a child, nurturing and bringing it up is an offering and a sacrifice to God. The altar is the family. Parents are the priests on that altar. The past and future have never fazed me. I was fond of only the present, the here and now.

I had chosen a monastic life and chastity while still living in this world, considering it as God's bidding. My life in its entirety was dedicated to Jesus Christ. Each of God's wishes was making me joyful. My heart was yearning for proximity with God.

The second year of the postulancy involved the study of the sacred scriptures and the liturgy. The shift from Koodathai to Dwaraka troubled me. The systems and practices there rankled me. On a number of occasions, there wasn't enough food. Even the portions were not set and varied wildly. Those who reached late had to go hungry. I was not able to reconcile to such an erratic system. Instead of protesting vocally, without seeking anyone's permission, I started to distribute the food set aside for the senior nuns to the others. I did this without being noticed.

The *maidan* alongside the convent was full of mango trees. Plucking and eating the ripe mangoes was forbidden. There was a similar edict against eating jackfruits that grew in the convent's compound. We were not permitted to talk to the nuns from other convents who were there to attend the retreat. I broke all three rules. I plucked and ate some mangoes. I savoured the honey-like sweetness of the jackfruit. I accosted guests, greeted them and chatted with them.

We had enough snitches among us to carry these tales to Mother Superior. That I hadn't been alone in these adventures is another matter. The mistress of the convent was a teacher. One of the sisters revelled in presenting our transgressions to the mistress as soon as she got back from work.

A trial was held. None of the co-conspirators owned up when we were asked about who had broken the rules; instead, they remained silent, with their heads bowed low. I stood up boldly and owned up to my actions. My punishment was to seek pardon on my knees. I couldn't convince myself that I had done something wrong. I remained still for a while, unable to decide what to do. I knelt down, raised my hands to the heavens and cried out. The sound of me crying breached the walls of the convent. My tears flowed uncontrollably and drenched my clothes. But they didn't accept my repentance.

When I came around after this long spell of crying, I offered a lengthy apology. For the next two to three days, I remained despondent. I thought that when Chachan came to see me the next time, I would go back with him—in the hope of escaping from my inner conflict by returning to my safe place, my home.

Chachan was ailing and undergoing treatment. However, he did appear on the usual day. As soon as they saw him, all the inmates of the convent acted as if nothing had happened and appeared cheerful;

no one complained about my behaviour either. I, too, forgot about all that had happened and became cheerful in his presence. He said his goodbyes when it was time, assuming that everything was all right.

The second year passed without further ado.

The venue for my novitiate, the final battle of my formation, was at Franciscan Clarist Congregation's St. Mary's Kunnoth convent under the Archdiocese of Thalassery. The vow of silence is a period of extreme asceticism and rigour. It is devoted to prayers. No contact with other nuns or family is allowed. When I led the prayers, I was complimented by everyone. After the peaceful period devoted to the vow of silence, I had to work in a hospital and an old-age home to gain experience in unsupervised, independent functioning. I was accompanied by two other novices. We carried out our duties competently and with dedication.

Chapter Five

ONE OF THE SUBLIME MOMENTS OF CONVENT LIFE IS WHEN YOUNG nuns profess the temporary vows—a public declaration of their commitment and intention to give themselves completely to God and to the service of others through the specific charism of the chosen order. It is the rarest of rare moments where one commits oneself fully and irrevocably to be the Bride of Christ. Members of one's family are present during this ceremony. It takes place in a spiritual ambience where faith and piety prevail.

I was well-served by the spirituality that I had discovered and distilled during my childhood and adolescence, and that energy filled me in my maidenhood. I had revelations through my dreams that made me certain I would find this salvation. Like the bride who yearned to be wedded, my soul pined to become a Bride of Christ.

> *We sing fervently to get through*
> *Flinty and thorny paths;*
> *To melt and wane*
> *And turn ourselves into unsullied oblation.*

Bearing candles in our hands, we sang these words in one voice. We prayed that our lives should culminate in a blaze of light and cheer.

In the company of my parents, dressed in a pure white saree and bearing a floral crown on my head, I walked in measured steps towards the stage. Many rituals during the service are symbolic of the solemn vows of chastity, poverty and obedience. During some of these, I imagined myself as a rose that had bloomed in the midst of my family, relatives and friends. It was a time of high emotion. Divesting oneself of the white raiment and donning a nun's habit was also a part of the ceremony. I, too, went through with it. I felt no difference inside me—only the colours of my clothing had changed. However, I was turned off by the ceremony's pomp and ostentation. My mind kept telling me that spiritual occasions should be shorn of such pageantry and spectacle.

Chapter Six

After I had completed my training, I was appointed as the personal assistant to the Provincial Superior of Assisi Bhavan—the provincial house of the Franciscan Clarist Sisters—at Malaparamba, near Kozhikode. This was my first appointment after I had put on the habit. I had to take care of the correspondence, which was the bulk of the work. I was also charged with receiving guests. The convent's inmates used to treat the nuns who came for sojourns as serfs. The partiality was there for everyone to see. I was, somehow, spared all this.

Across our convent was Christ Hall, a Jesuit retreat centre. One of its inmates came for a visit. The convent enjoyed cordial relations with the Jesuit brothers. I welcomed the brother, seated him and got busy making tea for him. I had also notified the sister he had come to meet. As I was boiling the tea, one of the inmates arrived and informed me that one of the sisters was asking for me. I told her that I would go as soon as I had served the tea. The guest gave me a thumbs up in appreciation. While in isolation it may seem trivial, this was an occasion when I became more aware of my fortitude. I was not one to regret the past or worry about the future. Neither of them perturbed me one whit.

I was at Malaparamba for only a year. I could choose any one of the three provinces of Malaparamba, Thalassery and Mananthavady. I had to settle on the field of my work and place of stay. I pondered deeply over the options; since Mananthavady was the least developed area, I chose it over the others. However, I came to understand that the Thamarassery Provincial Superior didn't like my decision much. I did realize that her displeasure was because I had chosen to move out of the province where I had started my life as a nun.

A little while after I joined Provincial House at Mananthavady, I got a chance to pursue higher education. Destiny brought me back to Nirmalagiri College for my undergraduate course in mathematics. Some of the other nuns from the convent were my classmates. While I was waiting in the queue for my admission, I was surprised to see Chachan ahead of me. He had come to get my younger brother admitted. Though I made no move to talk to him, when he turned around and saw me, he hurried towards me. Mother Superior was with me as my guardian to complete the college admission formalities. Waving off Mother Superior's protests, he then took over as my guardian. He paid the entire fee for my degree course. While he did this, he declared that he was happy to educate his own daughter.

During my undergraduate days, whenever there were extended holidays, I used to return to the Mananthavady convent. Onam and Christmas holidays were invariably spent in Karikkottakary. We were allowed to visit our parents once a year. However, there was a rule that we ought to spend the nights in the nearest convent. I never observed that rule. I took the decision to instead spend time with Chachan, who was ailing by that time. Only once did I spend the night in the nearby convent along with my sister who is also a nun. This happened during my first vacation after my temporary profession. Otherwise, my mother always insisted that I stay over for the night. Her argument was that I was sleeping at the convent every day and I could afford to sleep at home once in a while.

My undergraduate days were singularly incident-free. I used to take the help of an English professor, an older nun who was my roommate in the convent, to avoid the occasional skirmish. Since I liked to sleep, and sleep uninterrupted, I used to lie down beneath the bed during study time—sometimes even during the daytime. There were occasions when she was asked where I sat to study; she replied that I did it while lying under the bed. I never overcame my habit of falling asleep as soon as I started to read anything. In the end, however, I still managed to graduate in mathematics and score eighty per cent.

As I was getting ready to leave college, I became the object of lust for a nun from the Thalassery province. She used to treat me with special affection. She was very talkative and seemed to crave my company all the time. One night, under the guise of wanting to talk to me, she invited me to her room. She forced me to get into bed with her. I yielded with great hesitation and distaste. She fondled me and kissed me all over my body, thrusting her sexual desire upon me. For the first time in my life, at the age of twenty-four, I was the object of desire. I took a vow never to find myself in such a situation again.

After four years as a nun, I reached the Portiuncula FCC Generalate in Aluva for the next level of training. I was one in a batch of one hundred and one. Soon, I began to be recognized for my skill in preparing reports, which was part of the training. During the daily worship and prayers from 11 p.m. till midnight, most of the participants used to be half-asleep. Once, I chose not to take part in the Saturday night prayer. The punishment I received for this was an extra hour's worship the next morning.

When I returned after the training, the Provincial Superior of Mananthavady chose to interrogate me about my absence at the midnight prayers. However, the mission given by the Generalate to Mananthavady monastery ended without serious repercussions.

As if it were a reflection on the kind of answers I had given to their questions, plans were made to increase my experience in convent life. I had to begin work in three convents of Malappuram district and was made to do so for several weeks. This experience also opened my eyes to the groupism, internecine wars and the 'unity' in the convents.

After the completion of my studies, when I reached Mananthavady, the first attempt to send me for a teacher's training programme failed. I was responsible for making flower baskets for the altar, and I slowly got to know the members of the parish. I started to develop a special liking for a brother from the Congregation of St. Therese (CST Brothers). I continued to foster these feelings till my letter asking after his welfare fell into the hands of the Provincial Superior. I didn't feel that my natural feelings marred the soul. However, my case was presented before the Provincial Council as if I had been caught *in flagrante delicto,* or as if they were in possession of incriminating evidence. Though I was pronounced guilty at the time, I felt no guilt.

I couldn't join the BEd course the next year too.

I was going through a critical phase in a nun's life. I had to take part in a rigorous training programme to prepare myself for my Perpetual or Solemn vows. This was to take place in the Generalate in Aluva. We were a batch of about a hundred nuns. It was a period of extreme trial. There was no glamour or spectacle associated with the temporary vows ceremony. No relatives would be in attendance. This is one of the most sublime ceremonies in a monastic life. It is the holy day when one's worldly demise happens, and one dedicates one's life to humanity and God. I was selected to read from the Missal at Mass and I was complimented by all for my reading.

Chapter Seven

On my return journey home from Aluva, I could only reach as far as Malaparamba. Riots had broken out following former Prime Minister Rajiv Gandhi's assassination, and traffic had been disrupted. Chachan and my relatives had arranged a big welcome for me. He was saddened by my absence. When eventually I reached home a few days later, all I could see were the empty pots that once held the celebratory feast meant for me.

During those days, I was sent to join Dharmaram Vidya Kshetram (DVK), managed by the Carmelites of Mary Immaculate (CMI) order, in Bangalore for a one-year course in theology. I was selected as a guest student. After successfully completing the course, I returned to Mananthavady, only to join a BEd course in Hassan, Karnataka. There were three other nuns with me. We had to pay a donation of ten thousand rupees each to get admission.

During my studies there, daily worship at the church became irregular. As soon as I got back to the hostel, I would climb into bed and fall asleep. I felt I was being controlled by the other three nuns who were my friends and classmates. I would rise from the bed only when persuaded by them. In 1993, I graduated with a BEd degree in mathematics in the first class.

Within a few months of my return to Mananthavady, I found myself heading out again, this time out of the state. I had been appointed as the principal of a primary school in Bundi near Kota, Rajasthan, run by the Ajmer Diocese. Three sisters from Mananthavady Province were already employed there. I was chosen because the principal had to be a BEd degree holder.

Classes were run only till Class 3 in what was a very rustic area. I grew very fond of the children there. Hemant, Neha, Varsha, Vaibhav—all these kids were my pets. On Sundays and holidays I would visit their homes. After the daily teaching-related duties were over, I used to visit the homes of some good-hearted people to check on their welfare. I found great peace in these activities.

Our double-storey building was viewed with awe by the villagers. Initially there was some resentment towards it, but soon they all had a change of heart after our interactions with them. Then they started to view the convent and its inmates with sympathy tinged with pity for the nuns, for the life they had chosen to lead.

The manager of the school, a Goan priest, used to have his meals at the convent. His room, attached to the church, and the school building were adjacent to each other. Yet he seemed keen to spend as much time as possible with the nuns. When I declined his invitation to visit his room, I became a persona non grata to him. It didn't take much time for his antipathy to turn into open enmity. He started to humiliate and insult me openly. The nuns who visited his room became his darlings.

One day when I woke up, I found a feeling of fulfilment washing over me. The reason was a dream I had had some time during the night. In it, I was at a beautiful flower-strewn scenic spot by the riverside. It seemed to be the most peaceful place in the world. My reflection, in an angelic form, appeared in the smoothly flowing water. I could see Chachan at a distance, traversing what appeared to be the path to heaven. In the morning, after I awoke from this dream and had breakfast, Mother Superior walked up to me and informed me of Chachan's demise. I was stunned. It was one of the greatest tragedies of my life.

I was so numb that I couldn't even express my wish to see Chachan one last time. Mother Superior had no words of consolation for me. She said nothing. I was shattered. With telecommunication networks then not a tithe of what they are today, our convent and school didn't even have a telephone. Mother Superior kept pointing out the difficulty of reaching home immediately. She reminded me that the journey would be arduous—taking a bus or car from Kota to New Delhi, then getting on a flight from there—while highlighting the logistical problems associated with it and the travel time. Both the priest who had joined the dissuading party and Mother Superior were rather voluble in putting all this across to me. I was powerless and could not stand up to them. Grounded and silenced, I spent the days nursing Chachan's memories. They came roaring into my mind in unending waves. I shut myself off from everyone and spent a week in complete, self-imposed silence. Then my brother's letter arrived.

Though blocked arteries had troubled Chachan for long, he had always been bright and pleasant. There had been no physical weakness or debilitation. His busy involvement in solving his fellow men's problems had acted as an antidote to his ailment. Only days ahead of his death, he was involved in the construction of Valayam Road, which ran in front of our house. Kunjaanjaa's letter said that he had been in good health even during his last hours. It also spoke of how, in his dying moments, Chachan's facial expression and the twist of his lips seemed to be trying to pronounce Lucy *mol* (baby). His radiance didn't dim even after death. All of Karikkottakary and people from nearby villages had congregated at our house when his death was announced. Only I was missing.

I read the letter many times over. I could not convince myself just yet that Chachan was no longer in this world. Having missed the chance to have a last look at his body, I kept trying to force my mind to accept my bereavement. I managed to reach our home only on the forty-first day after my father's demise. I had to travel alone in the train. Mother Superior was not compassionate enough to assign a companion for me. During the angst-filled journey, the thought of Chachan kept me company.

I felt it was pointless to return to a home that no longer housed him. Everyone welcomed me with remorse. My mother remained brave. I was able to accept and adjust to his absence only after a few days. I had to return to Bundi before my period of mourning was truly over. I had not quite emerged from the grief. I tried to overcome my loss by getting closer to the students. I confessed my sadness to the Provincial Superior of Mananthavady during her visit to the convent. At that time, Ajmer Province was also under the Mananthavady Diocese. Along with her, I had an audience with the Bishop of Ajmer and I apprised him of my despondency. Following this, my return to Kerala was approved. This was around the time when we received another shocking news: that of the gruesome murder of Sister Rani Maria. She was an FCC nun killed on a bus in Indore in February 1995 by those who were opposed to her efforts in aiding the landless poor.

I returned to Mananthavady along with the Provincial Superior. This somehow made the nuns in the convent suspicious. I shared my troubles with the incumbent vicar general. While he was comforting me with his words, he also planted a kiss on my cheek before sending me on my way.

*

I was destined to undertake another sojourn far away from Mananthavady once again; this time I had to go to Surajgarh in

Jhunjhunu district of Rajasthan, very close to the state's border with Punjab. I was sent to a school there run by the CST order. I was despatched into this desert place as there was a vacancy for a mathematics tutor. Initially, I could not reconcile to this exile of sorts and protested. I was sent for a retreat to help me get over it. I finally left for Surajgarh, energized by the intense meditation and worship that I had undertaken.

I was given many responsibilities when I landed there. I carried all of them out with cheerful diligence. I was recognized in the church and the school. The convent had five nuns, of whom three were teachers, including me. The other two were involved in social service and I got along with them best. Concordance soon turned into friendship. However, the one-upmanship, egoism and interpersonal animosities in the other two inmates pained me. Soon, I became a persona non grata there too.

The school and the church were located close to each other, but the convent was a little further away. I had to teach mathematics to Classes 7, 8 and 9, and English to Class 2. Language was no barrier for me, so I could join in and contribute to the work being done among the parishioners. Learning the Hindi hymns by rote and reading out the Bible in Hindi, I soon became part of the group. I was also given church duties. My closeness to the villagers, and the enthusiasm and ease with which I mingled with them, caused envy among some nuns.

Though I recognized this, I wasn't ready to step back and turn into a silent painting on the wall. To be rendered mute and inert would move me away from God and experiencing divinity. One day, while I was setting up things for communion in one of the churches near the school, I noticed that I had forgotten to bring the sacramental bread. The priest and the devotees were already in the church for the service. I went up to the priest and confessed the failure on my part. He consoled me saying that the prayers can start with the rosary being said, and he informed the congregation of the change in the service.

In the days that followed, this very human failing of forgetfulness was, however, blown up as a mortal sin or worse. The main charge laid at my door was that I didn't inform Mother Superior first about my forgetting to bring the sacramental bread. Instead, I had revealed it to the priest. Mother Superior and her subordinate decreed that my manners and actions were not in keeping with the dictates of a monastic life. In reality, the camaraderie I had with the convent's other Malayali inmates was one of the reasons why these two disfavoured me. In a way, they were ostracizing me from the convent, at least in spirit.

The CST priest who managed the school treated me like his little sister. Though this was a matter of pride for me and a saving grace in the otherwise fraught atmosphere of the convent, I couldn't survive there much longer, and so I was back in Mananthavady after one year, with an unquiet mind. I had come to know that the Sacred Heart School in Dwaraka near Mananthavady had an opening for a mathematics teacher. So I grabbed this opportunity and fled from the agonies of life within the Kota convent, and from the region's extreme heat and cold, to the more pleasant clime of Wayanad.

Chapter Eight

Before joining the Sacred Heart School in Dwaraka, my temporary refuge was an unaided school in Kurumbala near Kuppadithara, run by the local church. My life in the monastery there was peaceful and to my liking. At the parish, I took up the duties of providing religious instruction and making home visits with enthusiasm. I accepted it as the realization of my monastic order. The appointment as the high school teacher at Dwaraka brought an end to my stint at Kurumbala.

When I reached the Provincial House, I received the order to join as a substitute mathematics teacher in a leave vacancy at the Sacred Heart School. I understood that the authorities were conflicted on the question of where I should be put up. When I demanded to know where my suitcases should be unloaded, I was told to head to St. Francis Convent in Dwaraka. The decision to send me there was a collective one, if not a conspiracy.

In a way, it was also my own decision to stay at Dwaraka, though. Two of my colleagues, both nuns, were also inmates of the convent. Though there were similarities between them, they were like chalk and cheese in many other respects.

The St. Francis Convent at Dwaraka is encircled by a number of other monastic buildings—such as the Pastoral Centre of the Eparchy; Vianney Bhavan, a sanctuary for elderly priests; Zion Charismatic Retreat Centre; and Family Apostolate. It is like a miniature version of Rome. The twenty-fifth anniversary of the monastery was celebrated around the time I started my stay there. I had joined the convent in December 1996 and the anniversary was celebrated the following year. I had provided leadership for some of the festivities. There were sizeable crowds of priests, nuns and laypeople in attendance.

My out-and-out efforts were appreciated. My capability and aptitude were there for all to see. That helped me advance in life some more. I became a member of the Youth Ministry initially and then of the Syro-Malabar Youth Movement/ Kerala Catholic Youth Movement, Dwaraka. The Youth Ministry led by Father George Moolayil used to conduct special catechism classes among the parishioners. In the bigger parishes, I was given the responsibility of conducting the classes. I was able to display my special skill in communication on these occasions. My work was acknowledged and appreciated. However, the energy and dedication I had displayed engendered jealousy in two of my companions in the ministry. They started a whisper campaign against me.

I was pained by the discord and disaffection within the convent. Gossip and obloquy against me were rife and rolled in wave after wave. My two teacher colleagues chose to join the opposition ranks. We used to walk from the convent to our school every day. On one occasion, a stray comment made by one of the sisters disturbed me. One of our acquaintances, a priest, had come over to speak to us when she remarked that a mouse had been turned back into a mouse (referring to the famous Panchatantra tale in which a sage is forced to turn a beautiful maiden back to her original mouse form). Subsequent events revealed that the mocking smile that the remark had brought on the acquaintance's face had, in fact, concealed many unsaid things. Little did I know that all along, my boldness grated on Mother Superior, who was also waiting for an opportunity to bring me down a few notches.

After a few months, Christmas was upon us. Christmas greetings were customarily exchanged in this convent in a particular manner. The inmates used to exchange cakes and wish each other Merry Christmas. Residents of other monastic institutions around us also went around doing the same, and our convent got eight cakes. My fellow nuns would gift the ones we received as presents to other institutions when we headed out to visit them. I objected to this. I proposed to the authorities that we should instead visit the houses of some of the indigents living near us and offer them these cakes, thus bringing them cheer and happiness. To those poor people, beloveds of Jesus Christ, this was an amazing and incredible experience. The words in the Bible announcing Christ's birth was what had inspired me to think differently.

> *Today in the town of David a Saviour has been born to you; he is the Messiah, the Lord. This will be a sign to you: You will find a baby wrapped in cloths and lying in a manger. Suddenly a great company of the heavenly host appeared with the angel, praising God and saying, 'Glory to God in the highest heaven, and on earth peace to those on whom his favour rests.'*
>
> Luke 2:11–14

When the next Christmas came around, I decided that the celebrations should be done differently. I selected the district hospital in Mananthavady as its venue. I planned everything and made a list of activities. Mother Superior approved them. She showed the large-heartedness to let me be me, and she accepted me for what I was.

The patients were amazed when we showed up and also by the gifts we presented them. When we greeted them, many broke into sobs. One of the novices from the convent had dressed up as Father Christmas. The priests and brothers from the neighbouring institution also participated with warm enthusiasm and full cooperation. This created a spiritual impetus in all of us. I had become the object of everyone's attention for having discovered the possibilities of celebrating Christmas differently and then putting it into tangible action. Unfortunately, the disaffection towards me also grew in similar proportion as a result of this attention.

Chapter Nine

In April 2000, there was a shake-up in the seats of power. A new provincial team took over. I was appointed as the Mother Superior of Alphonsa Balabhavan. Sister Jemma, the previous Superior at Alphonsa Balabhavan, a colleague of mine at the school who was later elected as a Provincial Councillor, worked behind the scenes to get me this honour. She sent me off with a gift, a new habit.

It was an orphanage with only seven girls as its inmates and was adjacent to the St. Francis Convent. The lady cook there resigned and left the day after I joined. I was unaware of what had made her quit, especially since she was close to Sister Jemma when she was the Superior at Balabhavan. Sister Jemma had succeeded in poisoning the girls' minds against me. She also spread calumnies against me among my colleagues in the school.

During my second year as the Balabhavan Superior, some new inmates arrived. We had children from different religions as inmates. Their lives before coming to us were wretched and pitiful. They were innocent victims of dysfunctional families and abusive households. One such child was a Class 9 student who used to work along with her mother as a housemaid after her father abandoned them.

Another one had survived an attempted murder by her own father, a deranged alcoholic. When she was asleep with her kid sister in their hut, he had attacked them with a knife. She had escaped by a hair's breadth; her sister didn't survive.

Though I liked to spend time and interact with the inmates, this was a time of disquiet. A controversy was created about non-Christians reading the Bible during worship. I was of the view that everyone should participate in the worship. However, one of the sisters who was assisting me opposed this. She had connections with my predecessor. They considered this a weapon to use against me.

They even misled the nuns who came as sojourners to the convent and turned them against me; I was branded as an insolent, defiant person. Whenever the duo got together, they would be whispering into each other's ears excitedly. One morning, I couldn't help being provoked by this behaviour. Threatening to put me in my place, they rushed towards me in response. I challenged them to do whatever they could and walked towards them. Overwrought and out of control, they cursed and swore. Though we didn't get physical, we were at each other's throats. Only once drained, we went our separate ways.

Though I was hurting inside and perplexed, I did go to the school. Soon afterwards, though, lies about me were publicized. The rumour that nuns had fought and I had set it off was bruited. I didn't bother to establish my innocence. I had the energy provided by the steadfast faith in truth and honesty that was ingrained in me. I also decided that I would not quail in the face of calumny and vicious gossip. Those were distasteful and angst-filled days. Words from the gospel fortified my self-belief:

> That's not the way it should be among you. Instead, whoever wants to become great among you must be your servant, and whoever wants to be first among you must be a slave to everyone,

> *because even the Son of Man did not come to be served, but to serve and to give his life as a ransom for many people.*
>
> Mark 10:43–45

A few days after the unwholesome incident, the provincial team arrived at the Balabhavan door. We were praying the rosary in the prayer room. There was a practice of locking up the door at a fixed hour every night. When the team arrived, one of the inmates came running for the key, which I used to keep. As soon as the door was opened, a group of seven nuns stormed in and entered my room. They locked the door from inside. And so my trial began.

I was charged with disobedience and insolence and quarrelling to boot. They read out the charge sheet that they had brought with them. They were demoniac and heavy-handed. They asked me to accept the charge sheet and sign it as proof of acceptance. Though I tried to read the words, nothing registered in my mind. I can't even recall now what mental state I was in then. I regained my equanimity and, summoning the spirit of forgiveness, I signed where they asked me to.

> *If your brother or sister sins against you, rebuke them; and if they repent, forgive them. Even if they sin against you seven times in a day and seven times come back to you saying, 'I repent,' you must forgive them.*
>
> Luke 17:4

Shining a big torch that could even have been used as a weapon, with haughty arrogance they stomped out of the place. I pondered over what is power and what is authority. I wondered whether power and authority had a place in monastic life. The motto of the FCC, 'To holiness through lowliness', is the order's hallmark and is representative of its regard for the meekest of the meek. In its essence, service is fraternity with the meek. Though I didn't despair, I wasn't contented either.

*

My concern for the children kept egging me on to advance my piety and love for my creator. An excursion I arranged for the orphans and children from broken homes to console and cheer them up turned out to be another gaping wound in my monastic life. A trip to Mysore had been planned and I had taken the required permissions from my superiors. The party consisted of the girl inmates, three nuns and Sheeba, the cook of Balabhavan, who had been appointed on my initiative. The vehicle for the trip was arranged by the headmaster.

We had completed all the arrangements on the previous day. We had cooked and packed breakfast and lunch for the day. Early in the morning of our departure, when I was getting ready, I received a message from the Provincial Superior asking me to cancel the tour. I suspected this was done at the last moment and out of spite, to show me in poor light before my wards.

I wasn't ready to abide by the order. I didn't share the news of this message with any of the others on the trip. I decided that I shouldn't be a killjoy and dampen the spirits of the children, who had been displaying especial energy and cheer ever since they were promised a pleasure trip. So we did go on the outing.

We reached the city after breakfast, halting for some tea, and started our sightseeing. I also didn't forget to distribute a little money among my wards for them to spend according to their liking.

Though they went to different schools, Sheeba's youngest daughter and my own brother's daughter were also part of the group. Only when we were about to return after a day of sightseeing did I remember that I hadn't given Sheeba any spending money. I made amends immediately. She took the money from me with apparent resentment, perhaps because I had missed her when I had given it to the children. I was disturbed by the look on her face, for I had never treated her as a cook and had always considered her my own sister.

Sheeba's husband had died by suicide. On top of her salary, she was given clothes, bags, umbrellas and other daily use items. I had imagined Balabhavan to be a house of love. Sheeba was considered a member of the family in that house.

On our return from the excursion, I had to face what was in a way extreme punishment. I realized that I was being singled out for a decision I had taken for the benefit of, and in order to not disappoint, the blameless children; I had no one to back me or speak on my behalf. I was once again accused of the grand sin of disobedience. When I had an opportunity to speak up, I told everyone the truth about how the decision had been announced at the last moment and I didn't have it in me to break the kids' hearts. Though no one challenged or refuted me, I could see that I was getting increasingly isolated.

The next morning, I got up late due to tiredness. The children were still sleeping. A message from the Provincial House had already reached Balabhavan. The nuns who had gone on the trip were asked to report at the Provincial House. The other nuns had left immediately. I was not prepared to go, leaving the exhausted children alone.

As soon as one of the 'antagonists' in the convent got back, I left for the meeting with the Provincial Superior, from whom I faced merciless fury and mistreatment. I was taken into a room and the door was shut behind me. With their sharpened weapons of interrogation and intimidation ready, the irate council members encircled me as if I was prey to be devoured. They shot their questions at me like a hail of arrows, not allowing me even to offer an answer.

Predictably, I went down silently, wounded in spirit. They insisted that I should sign the charge sheet they had prepared. I was not in the right frame of mind and could not manage to read the entire thing. However, one of the clauses caught my eye; had I signed it, I would be affirming that, having admitted to all my transgressions and errors, I was not fit for any position of authority. Summoning the last vestiges of my courage, I refused to bow down and said that I would never sign it.

> *[Pilate called together the chief priests, the rulers and the people and] said to them, 'You brought me this man as one who was inciting the people to rebellion. I have examined him in your presence and have found no basis for your charges against him.'*
> Luke 23:14

At this moment, when I thought I would sink and be overwhelmed, the words of Luke propped me up and gave me courage.

Their next decree was that I should return to the Generalate immediately. It was of no concern to them that I was a high school teacher. Their offer that I could continue there if I abided by their demands wasn't acceptable to me. After undergoing the uncivil interrogation in Balabhavan, this was the second shock for me. Two of the nuns who had accompanied me on the trip had to undergo harsh torture too. They were locked up for many days. They were let off only after they signed all the documents the superiors had placed before them. Though one of the nuns had accompanied us, by turning into a quisling and approver, she became the darling of the superiors.

Early the next morning, I left for the FCC Generalate in Aluva. The congregation of the provincial heads, including Mananthavady Provincial Superior Sister Rose Francy, was to commence that day. My objective was to meet the Superior General, unburden myself to her, and recover my peace and equanimity. I opened up to her without any pretences, and she consoled me and asked me to calm down first. She said the differences of opinion may have arisen because of some misunderstanding, and she assured me that she would ask the Provincial Superior to apologize to me. After I met her, the raging ocean inside me became calm.

I was permitted to participate in the retreat. I found a place only in the last row. Provincial Superior Francy, who met me there, apologized to me, smiled and embraced me. Before the retreat was over, I returned to Balabhavan as per the advice of the Superior General.

I felt much buoyed, as if I had returned to my own home. When I got back, Sheeba was missing. I was told that, from then on, she would be working in the nearby convent. We took up the slack, with the adults doing the cooking and the girls washing the dishes and cleaning up. The time spent with the children gladdened my heart.

In between all this, I arranged a study tour for Class 10 students from my school. We had decided on Thirunelli as the destination. Other teachers were going on the day trip too, and I invited Sister Vincy, an inmate of our convent, to join us. I wanted to provide her an escape from the terrible loneliness she was suffering in the convent. She happily accepted my invitation. But, at the bus station, we ran into Francy, who was on her way to Thalassery. She beckoned Vincy towards her and demanded angrily, 'Where are you off to? Go and sit in the convent.' Humiliated and broken-hearted, she had no option but to return to the convent.

One day, Jaicy Jose, a known antagonist of mine, did appear before me. She knelt down and apologized to me. She admitted to wronging me and spreading malicious rumours about me. On any given day, I used to keep her at arm's length. I avoided all conversations with her. This apology from her also didn't move me or help change my opinion of her.

Chapter Ten

After three years in Balabhavan, it was time for my next transfer. I was shifted to the convent where Sheeba was working now. I didn't tell anyone in my family what I was going through. When the Mananthavady Provincial Superior Sister Sinclare once came to Dwaraka, I broke into a flood of tears in front of her.

> *But you are not to be like that. Instead, the greatest among you should be like the youngest, and the one who rules like the one who serves.*
>
> Luke 22:26

During the next three years in the convent, I plumbed the depths of despair. My mind had become numb. I yearned for a break, if not a transfer. My Provincial Superior didn't stand in my way. I received her permission to attend the Consecrated Life course led by Father James Kannanthanam, who was the director then and is now the Provincial Superior of Claretians in Bangalore.

Life in Bangalore was cheerful and the climate pleasant, neither too warm nor too cold. However, the continuous hustle and bustle around me was suffocating. I desired solitude and used to lie on the flat roof of our building, surveying the magnificence of the skies. I saw the beauty of God in the stars, the conception of the divine caress—for all of nature was intoxicating.

Meanwhile, in Dwaraka, after I had taken a year's leave from my teaching duties for spiritual studies, I found that fresh allegations were being built up against me. The scuttlebutts originated from two of my colleague nuns who could see me only as an adversary. They spread the rumour that I had been sent to study as a punishment.

Back in Bangalore, during the training, as part of psychology, Father Kannanthanam asked me to undertake an exercise. As part of it, he presented a method of measuring the impetus in each of us to blame others. In this game-based exercise, there were forty participants. I failed when I was given the task of saying only bad things about each person in the group. I was fully worn down by the time I could get through ten. The priest, a psychologist himself, told us that this is a capability that is needed in certain situations in life.

> *Jesus answered him, 'I spoke openly to the world. I always taught in the synagogue and in the temple, where the Jews always meet, and I said nothing in secret.'*
>
> John 18:20

But I considered rumour-mongering a human frailty and among the basest of activities. During my childhood and adolescence, too, I couldn't inculcate this habit in myself. The root cause of all the trials and tribulations I had to undergo was jealousy and gratuitous malice. The majority of the nuns used to carry tales to parishioners' homes or to the priests. Those who didn't join them were seen as adversaries. That was how I ended up as everyone's bête noire and archenemy.

*

During our training, nuns and brothers used to stay in the same building within the compound. One night, as I was descending from the roof after enjoying the usual visions of the sky, I caught a movement from the corner of my eye. It was midnight, and there was a fellow trainee nun entering the room of one of the brothers.

I immediately informed Father James of this. To find out the truth, he knocked on that brother's door. The door was opened only after a few minutes. We could hear water falling into a bucket from inside the bathroom. To the question of who was inside, he answered that no one was there. Father James went into the bathroom and discovered the nun inside. He let them off with a warning. I decided I was not going to tell anyone, but I was turned off by the whole incident.

Then in 2004-05, during another training session in the Dharmaram Vidya Kshetram in Bangalore, I had the misfortune of witnessing a tragedy. It was a tale of sly perfidy. The victim was one of the nuns in my friends' circle. She had mentioned her upcoming trip to Bangalore in passing to a priest with whom she shared friendly relations. When she boarded the bus, she found him sitting in the seat adjacent to her. Apparently, he had managed to wangle a trip for himself to Bangalore at short notice. When the bus reached Mysore, he persuaded her to get off to have food. While she was eating, he went and booked a room in a hotel and then took her there. He had his fun and ended up having carnal relations with her. They took the next bus to Bangalore because they were going to the same institution. However, from the bus station, he arranged his own transport to his destination. And from then on, he treated her like a stranger.

The young sister went to pieces and came to me broken-hearted and agonizing over what had befallen her. I applied the balm of solace on her wounded heart and consoled her with calming words of comfort. I asked her to treat this as a lesson learnt and never to fall into such traps again.

After returning from Bangalore, I resumed my duties as a teacher in Dwaraka the following year. There were no drastic changes in the situation at the convent. My adversaries continued their sniping and backbiting. I was marooned in a sea of gossip and vilification and was increasingly isolated. Word spread that I was in love with a male teacher. We were good friends, and there was nothing beyond friendship. As the gossip became rife, he was shattered. He could recover and get on with his life only after meditation and counselling. The reins of this beast of vilification were held by the same cabal of nun friends of mine.

I used to be taken aback by their behaviour whenever we met. They used saccharine-coated words and embraced me as if we were long-lost friends meeting again. Their duality astounded me. They envied my friendship with my colleagues and any nuns new to the convent. On rare occasions, their resentment would burst out into the open. They would grumble and mutter, 'Does Lucy ooze honey from her pores?'

I realized that my desire to rise above everything and float like a butterfly in the firmament of social service was being trammelled. I wearied of the apostolic activities in Dwaraka getting vitiated through the disunity caused by the gossip and calumny. Fleeing to another remote place was the only way to escape my companions who revelled in the misuse of authority.

Chapter Eleven

In 2004, I was moved to Rajasthan and, in the company of five nuns, started a new convent there. The following year, I joined the English-medium school in Bhilwara under the Udaipur Diocese as a teacher of mathematics. In the convent there, the joy that Sister Meera brought to people who approached her was remarkable. Her grace and goodness stood out. But she was harassed for this very goodness, and after a few years of suffering through the torment, she left the congregation.

On many occasions there, I proved my own skill in communication—both to individuals and groups. In a matter of two years, I was able to build a productive and fulfilling life there.

The school had more than 1,500 children, in classes from kindergarten to senior secondary. Though the majority were local children, there were Malayali students too. Teachers were paid at government pay scales. The convent and a small church were adjacent to the school. The school office was staffed by Malayalis in important positions. I became close to the non-teaching staff, who were locals. I realized how tough their existence was and witnessed the privations they had to face. I tried to build strong bonds with such people.

On holidays, the local children used to come to the school grounds to play, dressed in torn and tattered clothes; I used to show them love and kindness. I would gather the children whose constantly running noses had permanently stained their faces. The convent inmates protested at my inviting these children in. They said they were repulsive. The priest, who was the manager of the school, was of a similar opinion.

I was a member of the prayer groups in Malayali homes. Priests didn't lead prayers on those occasions. Children used to read the Bible in their inimitable sing-song, lisping style. I enjoyed the prayers recited in Hindi. But the local priest's distaste towards my methods and style started to get more pronounced over time. I found I was again getting sidelined and isolated.

I was also troubled by the extremes of heat and cold there. A region with scant rainfall, it was bitterly cold from November to February. Thereafter it was blazing hot.

During the summers, classes started from 7.30 a.m. Though classes got over at 1 p.m., going out into the heat of the afternoon was unthinkable. The only option was to sleep in the convent due to the heat exhaustion. The local denizens used to sleep either on the roof of the house or in the courtyards. On one hot day, I had gone to the convent early and was charged by the manager-priest with the offence of leaving the school premises without permission. After completing two years, I decided to quit my job in Bhilwara and rejoin the Sacred Heart School in Dwaraka. However, the hierarchy in Rajasthan was not ready to accept my resignation. I stuck to my decision and came away to meet the Superior General at Aluva.

Chapter Twelve

Once back in Mananthavady, I settled into a non-confrontational lifestyle, avoiding controversies and conflict. My twenty-fifth anniversary as a nun was approaching. A simple ceremony marked the occasion in the Provincial House, where I was an inmate at the time. A communal prayer was organized, and my friends and comrades from other provinces participated in it. Though I was not given the charge of making the arrangements, I started as a locum in catechism classes for Class 1 students. As I was leaving for the first day of classes, I was accosted by Assistant Provincial Superior Jincy with these jealous words: 'Ah, you are going to shine a little too much, aren't you?'

After almost two and a half years, my next sojourn was at Kavumannam, in Kerala's Wayanad district, where I stayed and did evangelical work while still teaching at the Sacred Heart Higher Secondary School, Dwaraka. Regi Muthukathani was the priest at the local church. I joined him and the convent's inmates in apostolic activities. I was recognized for my contributions to catechism classes, training children in Bible reading, the choral group, family unit and the church youth organization, and was given sufficient latitude by the priest. For about a year and a half, activities went on with effortless ease.

But conflict continued to brew underneath all this. It reached a flashpoint over a certain child's non-inclusion in the chorus, which the parish priest protested against. I was then removed from the Christmas Day Mass choral group without notice, though it was my third Christmas there. There were other complaints foisted on me too. Until then, our relationship had been very cordial and amiable. I could not understand what had changed and why it had changed. I kept trying to find out the real cause of his displeasure. The only reason I could think of was my telling someone who had once come in search of the priest that I didn't know where he was.

On Christmas Day, my mind seared with anguish when I went to the dining room and saw him seated there, having food. He insulted me there too. I was burning with humiliation and shame. I cried out loudly, and my cries broke through the convent walls. None of the inmates, including the Mother Superior, had anything to say to me in my moment of mortification. I do not remember how long I kept crying. I decided that I would not remain there any more.

When I reached the Mananthavady Provincial House, I was greeted by resentful, scowling faces. They were ruthless and graceless in their behaviour. I could make out from their expressions that they believed I had come back after picking a fight with the parishioners and priests.

*

Shortly thereafter, I was transferred to the FCC convent in Kommayad, only three kilometres away from my school in Dwaraka. By now, I no longer had any false notions that I would win either respect or appreciation. The convent had four nuns. The building was in a dilapidated condition. We worked together and succeeded in getting things into some form of order. Sister Sincy Mathew was the Superior of the convent. She was younger than me. Though our diet was pre-decided and food prepared jointly, it was found that there were many slips between the cup and the lip. The rest of them decided that a certain Sister Philcy and I had ganged up. The Superior took charge of the kitchen and the provisioning. Things came to such a pass that on many nights Philcy and I had to go to bed on an empty stomach.

Sincy was an out and out miser. In my twenty-five years as a nun, I had never had to experience such paucity of food. Convents usually have well-stocked larders and feed their inmates well. We used to be served fish and meat and the food was generally tasty. Rare were the occasions when there was a disruption. These rare occasions only came when the authorities would, out of the blue, start to feel that Christianity was under strife or passing through a crisis. Their knee-jerk reaction on such occasions was to instruct the flock to eschew what were considered excesses and luxuries in their book. It was then that the provincial superiors would think up ways to comply with such edicts. Most of the time, though, the restrictions imposed would be limited to inmates making do with a simple diet devoid of non-vegetarian dishes. Unfortunately, at the receiving end of these decisions were the poor, long-suffering nuns. Such decisions are inspired by cretinous beliefs that the spiritual energy that comes by fasting and starvation is what is needed to overcome the crises faced by Christianity and the Church from time to time.

In general, though, since convents served wholesome food, nuns were usually healthy. Therefore, the dearth of food, let alone nutritious food, at the Kommayad convent was of great concern. Philcy was ailing, and since she had to take medicines often on an empty stomach, she had complications and grew weaker over time. There were occasions when, to assuage our hunger, we had to buy tapioca on the way back from school, boil it and eat it without a dip or side dish.

The convent building was old. Only two rooms had doors, one of which was appropriated by the Superior for her use. The other was a dark, dingy one with no ventilation. So the rest of us used to sleep in the hall. All visitors had to pass through this hall. The Superior's ways were strange and insufferable. In a convent, usually nothing is locked up; rooms are left open. But she kept her room locked up. She used to pick up every scrap and junk found by the roadside and keep it in her room. It was a proper junkyard and a dumping ground rolled into one and used to smell like one.

*

Though there was no mental peace, I continued to move closely with the parishioners and kept up my friendship with them. It was a relief and some respite from the enervating and nauseating life in the convent.

Once I went to a sickly parishioner's house to take care of him. With his elephantiasis in advanced stage, he was in a pathetic condition. I suggested ways to proceed with his medical care. As part of the treatment, a huge chunk of flesh was removed from his leg. On his return from the hospital, I began to visit him almost daily. He was so lonely that to meet and talk to anyone was a mercy and a solace. However, the Superior and others frowned upon such humanitarian actions of mine. Though the Church had given him some money for his treatment, it too chose to turn its back on his mental rehabilitation.

Another time, one of three sons of a farmer from the parish killed himself, throwing the family into deep despair. I realized they needed someone to lean on, someone to prop them up, or they would collapse. I interacted with them continuously until they could reconcile with and recover from their loss.

Once, an upstanding member of the parish, an autorickshaw driver by profession, died suddenly. A hardworking man, his heart suddenly stopped pumping when he was driving his vehicle. Though he was rushed to the hospital, he couldn't be revived. His children were still students—the elder one in senior secondary and the younger one in high school. The construction of his house hadn't been completed. The family was reaching out for any solace they could receive. I reached out to them, comforted them, prayed with and for them for many days. All of this invited the disapproval of the Superior.

> *The King will reply, 'Truly I tell you, whatever you did for one of the least of these brothers and sisters of mine, you did for me.'*
> Matthew 25:40

These words from the holy book stood me in good stead during those testing times.

The purpose of a monastic life is to gather to the rebuffed and spurned lives and to keep them in a close embrace. I set out on this life path, attracted by the mission of keeping close to oneself those in sorrow and in pain and providing them comfort and succour. I had implicit faith in my purpose. I wasn't overly concerned by the nit-picking or petty aversions of the convent's authorities. In the meantime, their animosity towards me kept increasing.

The Provincial Superior, Sister Stephina, visited me in the convent. She spoke to me alone in the chamber and hinted about a transfer. I told her without mincing my words that unless the cause and rationale were explained to me, I would not comply with any of their directives.

Chapter Thirteen

In March 2014, I was deputed to St. Joseph's Higher Secondary School in Kallody, roughly seven kilometres from Mananthavady and eight from Kommayad, for invigilation duty for the Class 10 public examinations. We were four invigilators in charge of the IT examination. Twelve computers had been set up in a classroom. The invigilators had the power to assign marks for the examination. In the normal course of things, no one was failed in this examination; the marking was liberal.

On the first day itself, there was an untoward incident. The headmistress of that school, who was serving as the chief examiner at the time, alleged that three students of her school were given lower marks than they merited. Though a revaluation was done, none in our group was willing to change the marks that had been assigned. The headmistress and some teachers of that school demanded that the examination be postponed. When their demand was not accepted, their intimidation tactics began. They threatened they would fail the students of my school, as teachers from their school were invigilators in our school. We were not swayed by that either.

On the second day, things took a different turn. The school took a stand that unless the marks were increased, they would not let the exams proceed. Halfway through, they chose to turn away the students who had queued up to enter the examination hall.

We were left with no option but to notify the District Education Officer (DEO), who was responsible for the proper conduct of the examinations. I informed him over the phone that the school authorities were not permitting the students to attend the examination. I also explained the incidents of the previous day to the officer. We were left waiting in the examination hall for the students to turn up. In the meantime, the DEO's call to the headmistress and his directive to continue with the examination were effective. She complied.

Soon the DEO came in person and made enquiries. After reissuing the orders to continue with the examinations, he suspended the headmistress from public examination duties. Since I was already in the bad books of the convent authorities, this incident at Kallody added fuel to the fire. Though there were four of us, all the blame was foisted on me; it was easy to do so as I was the senior-most staff member there. Our stand during the examination was unanimous. It was a group decision and I was only a member. Though the conspirators managed to instigate some children to petition against me to the DEO, it came to nought.

> *It is for freedom that Christ has set us free. Stand firm, then, and do not let yourselves be burdened again by a yoke of slavery. Mark my words! I, Paul, tell you that if you let yourselves be circumcised, Christ will be of no value to you at all. Again I declare to every man who lets himself be circumcised that he is obligated to obey the whole law. You who are trying to be justified by the law have been alienated from Christ; you have*

> *fallen away from grace. For through the Spirit we eagerly await by faith the righteousness for which we hope.*
>
> Galatians 5:1–5

The disgraced headmistress was a close friend of one of my adversaries, Sister Pavana, a Provincial Councillor. This nun asked me to withdraw the complaint against the conduct of the examination. As I had not lodged any written complaint, I was not ready to accept this. The Kallody school was one among the many under the corporate school system run by the Mananthavady Diocese. The system turned on me with its full might; the moves against me grew stronger. During those dark days, I had to go through many strange and untoward experiences. I received phone calls from our monastic order, the school management and teachers' organizations directing me to withdraw the complaint. I, however, was not ready to side with dishonesty and injustice and yield to them. Though I was put under tremendous pressure, I could not find any cause or reason to change my stance on the issue.

The Provincial Superior called me and ordered me to appear before her in Mananthavady. The scornful phrases she used to summon me caused me great mental agitation. I replied that since examinations were on, and I was staying at the convent in Kommayad, I wouldn't be able to go there immediately.

Chapter Fourteen

THE PROVINCIAL SUPERIOR CAME TO THE KOMMAYAD CONVENT, where I lived in oppressive circumstances, to meet me in person. She had come to sound me out on a transfer for me. I told her categorically that inopportune transfers would be inconvenient. I was not ready to accept the offer. When the Assistant Provincial suggested that it was God's will that a transfer was taking place, my counter was that my standing up to the transfer was also God's will. They were in no position to order me about.

There were many reasons for my demurral. Many of the sisters who have set out on the path of monastic life have had to face many difficulties from these untimely transfers. The wanton exercise of power, based on pure whim, has culminated in some of the subjects almost quitting the cloister. Those who hold power and are in positions of authority completely fail to notice the wounds they cause to their own wards and colleagues.

The convents have set timings for reading notifications of transfer and similar official letters. This practice is in place to ensure transparency in internal procedures. The contents of my transfer order to Dwaraka were already known to the priest and Mother

Superior. The priest wasted no time in spreading the glad tidings of my departure, with the Superior chiming in where needed. While there was a chasm between the vicar and me, the parishioners had no such reservations and were quite friendly with me.

The young vicar seemed to resent the fact that I showed no inclination to get close to him. Though I was aware of this, I stuck to my path of righteousness.

*

I was in the habit of giving benediction to children and to adults after conducting prayers in parishioners' homes. By keeping my hand on the believers' foreheads, I used to pass on the benediction and godliness that I had accumulated. Many of them have told me of the transformations they have undergone as a consequence. Some of them testified that they were cured of their pain; some found relief from ailments.

In an open declaration of his antipathy towards me, the young parish priest, Isaac (Sunil) Vattukunnel, sent me instructions that blessing people by touching the foreheads should not be done by nuns. In his opinion, that was trespassing into priests' territory and usurping their divine rights. Envious of my popularity and acceptance among the parishioners, he sent spies who would watch me and report to him. Sometimes, he himself set out to perform his iniquitous activities.

Though not as some kind of admission of the primacy of priests, I gradually gave up the practice of giving benediction by touching believers' foreheads openly. I decided to restrict the practice to only those very close to me. I have blessed my colleague teachers and even the principal, providing them with relief during stressful days at work. I have my doubts about this priest's understanding of divinity because he didn't value what was clearly God's work. In this, I am a representative of womanhood, which is constantly humiliated by being undervalued.

> *[It is God's will that you should be sanctified: that you should avoid sexual immorality;] that each of you should learn to control your own body in a way that is holy and honourable, not in passionate lust like the pagans, who do not know God; and that in this matter no one should wrong or take advantage of a brother or sister. The Lord will punish all those who commit such sins, as we told you and warned you before. For God did not call us to be impure, but to live a holy life.*
>
> Thessalonians 4:4–7

The priest was eventually transferred elsewhere after incurring the displeasure of the parishioners.

Then there was another vicar, whose speeches initially were loaded with spirituality. However, he was excessively fond of girls; I couldn't help but notice that he seemed keen to be in feminine company all the time, though I didn't pay much heed to it. The other nuns from the convent were, however, acquiescent. The girls in the church choir were also his targets; he showed undue interest in them. The doors of his room were always open to them; he invited them and pressed on them to visit him. The ones who went to him were caressed and petted.

> *And do not let sexual immorality, or any impurity, or greed be named among you, as these are not proper among saints. Let there be no filthiness, nor foolish talking, nor coarse joking, which are not fitting. Instead, give thanks. For this you know, that no sexually immoral or impure person, or one who is greedy, who is an idolater, has any inheritance in the kingdom of Christ and of God.*
>
> Ephesians 5:3–5

On one of the days of the church festival, when I was passing behind his room, I saw him embracing one of the girls rather tightly. As soon as he saw me, he moved away from her. Under such circumstances, I should have called and counselled that girl; it was remiss on my part that I didn't do so. The girl I had seen was from a rich family, well educated and beautiful. I, for some reason, didn't feel the need to advise her. I also didn't inform anyone about the unchaste acts of the vicar. Very soon, he was also transferred out of the parish. We came to know that this was the result of a petition that the parishioners had submitted directly to the bishop.

*

A remarkable capacity for independent thinking and action had grown in me. I either inherited or assimilated it from my circumstances. Even when I was in strife, I depended on no one for my decisions; every decision was taken by me. At the right time, the appropriate conclusions for my next step and the way ahead used to become clear in my mind.

I also didn't inform my family of the goings-on in the convent, whether favourable or unfavourable. I was loath to share my experiences with anyone, let alone my family. My family also respected my reticence. Almost all members of the Kalapurakkal family were born self-reliant. No one wanted to impose decisions on others or liked to have decisions imposed on themselves.

Thanks to my resistance, my transfer was delayed by a year; eventually, I was transferred to the FCC Convent, Karakkamala, in Wayanad district. There was no pomp and ceremony, no fanfare; my transfer was effected quietly. I was already marked out as a problem person. Rebellion against authority was in my blood; it was ingrained in me. My faith in Jesus Christ was steadfast and unimpeachable.

My quarrel was only with acts that were dishonest and reeked of doubtful integrity.

The lessons I learnt from my stormy, combative monastic life didn't transform me. I was unable to cry over the past or feel vain about it. I couldn't find any act in my life as a servant of God that needed redemption. The initial days in Karakkamala were not unfulfilling or unsatisfactory. Counting Mother Superior, there were seven of us in the convent. In the first few days, I realized that one of the nuns, Sister Carmaly, would be joining the growing ranks of my adversaries.

An inveterate tattletale, she has played an important, if toxic, role in my life, along with two other nuns. To my face, she was always sweet and unctuous; she praised me to the heavens. She tried to win me over with her honey-coated words. However, whenever I was out of earshot, she disparaged me, cast aspersions and showed her envious spitefulness.

I was given the charge of running the catechism classes for Class 10 students. The conduct of family units, animation of the youth movement, Eucharist adoration and the training of children in Bible reading thus became my responsibility. Three of the inmates, including me, were teachers. The others were involved in parish services. Sister Lissy was genial and amiable to everyone. She was older than all of us. I was always at her service and happy to aid her. She used to be an early riser and the first to be in the church for the rosary—in this, I always gave her company, as the other nuns were invariably late.

Chapter Fifteen

It was during those days that the news about Bishop Franco of the Jalandhar Diocese began to emerge. Television was the main medium through which news from outside reached the cloisters. Only the Provincial Generalate had access to a multiplicity of newspapers. All the convents received only *Deepika*, a daily newspaper owned and published by the Syro-Malabar Church. No one showed any interest in reading this paper. The little interest shown was confined to scanning the headlines and gazing at the pictures.

None of the clergy was interested in knowing what was happening in society. Everyone was interested only in spiritual matters, but even that was done mechanically. The Church also decreed this. No one baulked at the idea of complying with such infantile orders.

Yet the campaign by a nun against Franco made all of us uneasy. However, we all had very different viewpoints. I saw it as a sexual assault on a helpless and defenceless woman. I was enraged by the approach taken by the Church towards the complainant. I could only see it as denial of justice to a forlorn, powerless woman. I could see that the Church authorities were trying to pass off this crime as a product of enmity towards Christianity and the Church;

they were trying to frame it as an act of religious hatred. Within the Church, the belief was that the complaint arose from animosity towards the Church.

At our convent, the talk around the dining table mirrored the stance taken by the Church, I being the sole exception. The other residents willingly swallowed the spiel fed to them by the Church authorities, hook, line and sinker. They also vocally expressed their opinions along these lines. They blamed and cursed the TV presenters and news anchors. The nuns branded them as muckrakers out to slander the Church. None of them had a whit of empathy for the nun, one of their own fellow sisters who was compelled to complain as she was at the end of her tether. One of the often-heard arguments from the nuns was: why had she allowed herself to be taken advantage of, no less than thirteen times, despite knowing him to be a sexual predator. They were conveniently completely ignoring the low position she occupied in the power structure of the Church's hierarchy, the misgivings she would have had about people believing her, as it was her word against that of a prelate, and many such imaginable and unimaginable constraints she had to battle.

I was determined that I should stand with this isolated soul. It was a logical and natural conclusion as far as I was concerned. I was only heeding God's wish to support those who are in trouble and in mourning.

*

I had a fairly good understanding of the use, power and reach of social media. I realized it had to be the channel to show my solidarity for my wronged sister; I began to post regularly on Facebook in her support. When this gained attention and traction, reporters from the Asianet TV channel came to our school.

In the meantime, a group of sisters started a sit-in protest at Vanchi Square near the High Court in Ernakulam, demanding justice for the persecuted nun. I decided to back those nuns who were fighting injustice. I also decided that I should go there in person and thought up a ruse to do it. I had to do it this way because I was afraid that my move would be thwarted if it were publicly known. I declared that I was visiting my brother residing at Kalamassery near Ernakulam. Though the convent authorities may have suspected something, they didn't oppose my trip.

The TV team came in the afternoon of the day I was planning to leave for Ernakulam. I spoke to them frankly about my stand on the whole issue. I had no misgivings or anxieties in relation to opening up. I was speaking to society at large with a clear mind. I had grown to realize that true service to God lies in such honesty.

I had reserved a seat in a private bus. I was cheerful when I headed to the convent from the school. By then, my interview had been telecast by the channel. Many who were sympathetic to my stand and supported it called me on the phone. They requested me to participate in the evening talk shows on some TV channels. I agreed without any hesitation. I would have to make a pit stop at one of the TV studios before heading to Ernakulam.

Just as I was leaving for my trip, one of the sisters sarcastically said, 'Oh, now we'll have to watch the TV to catch a glimpse of you.' I understood that either the inmates had watched the telecast or someone from outside had apprised them of it. It was not as if I was the first person from the Syro-Malabar congregation to appear on TV or talk shows—for one, Father Paul Thelekkat was a regular on TV channels.

The inmates had little interest in watching the news. The majority of them watched only the never-ending serials on TV. These tear-jerkers held no interest for me, nor did I find time to watch these serials, the unchanging themes of which were illicit relationships and duplicities in families. Neither did the thunderous evangelism of Shalom TV move me.

I left the convent by 7.30 p.m. and reached the channel's Kalpetta studio via the vehicle arranged by them. I replied to the talk show host's questions without prevarication and boldly proclaimed my support for and solidarity with the victim. Then I left for Kalamassery in a bus arranged by the channel. I went to my cousin's house along with my relatives who received me. From the time I had made up my mind to join the sisters' protest, my mind was wholly preoccupied with their struggle. I found it impossible to accept my relatives' suggestion to take a little rest.

I had my bath and change of clothes and headed to the protest *pandal*. I touched the hands of each sister participating in the sit-in by the roadside as the milling crowds passed by them. I felt as if I had been sanctified. The determined looks in their eyes flowed into me as pure energy. That was enough to banish the smidgen of qualms in my mind. I felt my mind clearing up and turning into a brilliant white sky. I held long conversations with those present. For me, each word was pregnant with passionate intensity and every sentence bore the heartbeat of Jesus Christ.

I was very animated and forgot that I had had no food. I was with the sisters till 4 p.m. My visuals were all over the TV channels. I thought I should spend one more day with them.

I was never worried about the future, nor was I nervous about anything. I always used to live in the present and for the present day. Nevertheless, my relatives were unduly worried and fell prey to some irrational fear. I had to bow to their insistent wishes and abandon the idea of spending the second day with the sisters. Instead, I continued to lend my support to them through social and mainstream media in the next few days.

*

In the meantime, the Superior at the convent and the Church hierarchy had come to know of my presence in the protest *pandal* from the TV reports. When I called the convent to inform of my return plans, the Superior asked me at what time they could expect me. I told her I would reach by early morning the next day.

When I entered the convent the next day, after taking the night train from Ernakulam, I was greeted by the voice of the Superior asking me to meet her. Tired from my journey, I told her that I would go to her after getting some rest in my room. Without much keenness, I told her once more that I shall be back and headed for my room. Once in my room, I thought that I shouldn't procrastinate; instead, I should let her tell me whatever she had to convey.

> *Truly, truly I say to you, unless a grain of wheat falls into the ground and dies, it remains alone. But if it dies, it bears much fruit.*
>
> John 12:24

I returned to present myself before the Superior and expressed my readiness to hear what she had to tell me. She told me that I had been replaced in the catechism class and that I needn't be involved in the Eucharist or the distribution of the sacramental bread. I offered no reply and sat quietly, listening. She also conveyed that I needn't lead prayers in the family units or get involved in the youth group activities. As I began to rise without replying, she said that it was an order. I asked her whose order it was, and she replied it was from the local church.

The vicar was Stephen Kottakkal, who had recently returned from a three-month visit to England. I was surprised by and had doubts about the order issued by someone who hadn't gathered first-hand information. When I went to the church for mass, I didn't take my usual place at the front of the altar but stood in the last row. Sensing something was amiss, some of the youngsters wanted to get to the bottom of it. I myself felt no inconvenience.

I had become news in the school and among the parishioners. My colleagues complimented me when I reached the school the next day. The students looked on in admiration. My removal from parish services didn't affect me in any way. In the meantime, a support group was formed in my name in Karakkamala among the believers. The Provincial Superior and the vicar issued a press release. It announced my removal from various responsibilities citing my contra-monastic life as the cause.

Once this was made public, there was immense pressure from the faithful in my support. Their message reached the bishop. Though the press release wasn't withdrawn, they were forced to announce that the actions against me had been withdrawn. The laity outside celebrated the failure of the cabal's attempt to divest me of my responsibilities. They claimed that the faithful had won a battle for freedom. Many others celebrated in silence when vindictive acts against me didn't succeed. I understood that, in their circumstances, they couldn't afford to be vocal about it, and they were, even in their silence, lending me support.

Chapter Sixteen

FOLLOWING THESE INCIDENTS, THE MOOD IN THE CONVENT CHANGED. Everyone stopped talking to me. I became an outcast as everyone deferred to the orders passed on to all convents and monasteries in Kerala. The Church authorities' intention and strategy was to isolate me completely. They believed that I wouldn't be able to survive the insufferable silence around me. Instead of following the routine of convent life, I set my own agenda—even deciding my own dining and sleeping hours. Every obstacle also seemed to suggest a way to overcome it. I was turning more energetic and becoming bolder.

My life seemed to be split into two halves—one, before declaring my solidarity with the Missionaries of Jesus sisters at Vanchi Square, and the other after that. Despite their shunning of me, I hadn't stopped trying to converse with the other nuns at the convent. Whatever I needed to know, I would ask them. Though some of my questions went unanswered, some of them received monosyllabic replies. They tried not looking at me or meeting my eyes. However, I wasn't fazed; one day, with my face incandescent with rage, I asked Sister Carmaly: Shouldn't they stop the charade?

Sister Joslin, a seventy-four-year-old blameless sister, had gone a step further than all the others; in a voice that betrayed desperation, she had asked me if I couldn't just leave the convent and leave them to lead their peaceful lives. As I was fed up with their immoral stance, I told her in a loud voice that maybe she should leave instead of me.

Ostracized in the convent, I continued to attend mass at the church. The vicar never attempted to hide his displeasure. From the pulpit, he held forth on my failings. All the other churches in Kerala heard similar homilies. The propaganda was intended to misinform and turn the believers against me. However, subsequent events revealed that they didn't succeed entirely.

The religious teachers and their custodians were angry with me and their interactions showed this. The vicar decreed that only he and Mother Superior should distribute the Eucharist. In breach of that, I used to walk up to the altar along with Mother Superior. Though they made their annoyance apparent, I behaved as if I had never noticed it. Many of the devotees sided with me. Eventually, to be freed from the rebuff, I dropped all my pretences of toleration. Another person was appointed so that I could be removed fully from catechism class duties. I wasn't affected in the least by these shenanigans. I preferred to believe that Jesus Christ loved it this way.

Chapter Seventeen

I IGNORED THE WHOLE CONVENT'S BEHAVIOUR TOWARDS ME. BUT I HAD to appeal to the authorities to extend financial help of ten thousand rupees for someone who was a well-wisher of my family and close to us. They rejected it summarily. After three decades of life as a nun, this was my first request; the reply astonished me. I had never, until that point, asked for any help from the congregation in relation to any personal need. I had not begged for help for anyone in my family or for any outsider. I found it risible that the reason cited was that my application was unclear. This stance of theirs deepened my division with them. With their heartless rejection of that appeal for help, I understood what their agenda was.

Subsequently, I wanted to get a driving licence—a wish that was not born out of a whim. Whenever the convent inmates had to travel, they had to depend on priests on most occasions. We had to travel in their vehicles or in the vehicles arranged by them—often an uneasy proposition. A few of us decided that we should learn driving to avoid such instances. When I applied for permission, I didn't receive a response either way. I was angered at the injustice of denial through inaction. It should not be overlooked that nuns were already learning to drive vehicles for the needs of their own institutions.

Considering that I was a socially productive teacher of good standing in the socio-religious and educational sphere, I was unable to bear the injustice shown to me. I mused about the kind of injustice that other sisters of the order engaged in social service would be undergoing if this was the case with me. The nuns were not in any position to ignore or challenge the edicts of the authorities.

I decided to go ahead with my decision. I joined a driving school not far from the convent and started taking lessons. At this point, moves to target me were also afoot in the school. A new manager had taken over, replacing the previous troublemaker. Not that I had much hope, but I made a few attempts to speak frankly with the new manager. Though he did not give opportunities in the beginning, I persisted and created one and we had a talk. His reaction was amiable.

Chapter Eighteen

THE SACRED HEART HIGHER SECONDARY SCHOOL AT DWARAKA, founded by Father Mathew Kattady in 1983, was not managed by the Mananthavady Eparchy but by the Norbertine Congregation of Thalappuzha. His entry into Wayanad has a backstory. He came as an aide to Mar Jacob Thoomkuzhy, who was the first bishop of the Mananthavady Eparchy. Hailing from Changanassery, he was specially invited by the Church to come to Mananthavady.

He was assigned with a specific mission to the Norbertine Centre that had only two German priests and some custodians to aid them. A seminary was being run in Norbert House at Kuzhinilam. Father Kattady, engaged in the management of the seminary, put forth the idea of a school in Wayanad. Realizing that the area between Mananthavady and Vellamunda lacked a high school, he made a case before the authorities of the eparchy and highlighted the prospects of getting the necessary approvals for the construction of the school. The eparchy showed little interest. Therefore, Father Kattady took the task upon himself.

His father, an educationist and a public worker, was also the principal of a reputed educational institution in Changanassery. He had close connections with leading politicians in the state, especially the then Minister of Education P.J. Joseph. Using these contacts and influence, they started to make attempts to open a high school in Dwaraka. A farsighted man with sterling values, Father Kattady was aware of his ordained mission as a priest.

They headhunted and brought in good teachers and appointed Sister Sinclare of FCC as the first headmistress. Father Kattady had laid down some basic principles for the running of the school. One of the main ones was that no money would be taken in the guise of donation or for making appointments. Only those with proven pedagogical skills were accepted as teachers. For the non-teaching staff also the principle of merit was used.

Father Kattady had definite ideas about the school. Even the design of the school buildings was first drawn in his mind. He was very attentive to the development of infrastructure and acquisition of amenities in the school. He used to refer to the incomplete building as his darling daughter. He used to take care of the school as a father would his own family.

Pointing to the incomplete building, he would compare it to a seventeen-year-old daughter. 'She is not lovely enough; a *bindi* has to be applied on her forehead; ornaments should be worn by her; she must be properly made up into a comely maiden. I am on the lookout for a suitable boy for her.' Truly, the school was his family.

Another time he said, 'We have an elephant. She needs a bell on her neck to tinkle as an accompaniment to her stately gait. We must tie a bell that will swing and ring.' When he made such allusions in his own style with rhythm and alliteration, none of the listeners would have any doubts about what he was referring to.

As long as he was managing the school, everything functioned like clockwork. After a while, there was a dispute about the ownership of the school. The eparchy filed a suit against Father Kattady. He joined issue with them in the court. At his advanced age, he was finding it difficult to run the school as before all by himself. There was also a shortage of funds.

To stop the bleeding and to find money to pay back the loans, Father Kattady eventually decided to transfer the ownership of the school to the Norbertine Congregation. He assumed that during the twilight of his life, the congregation would take care of him. With the belief that his last days would be spent there, he even had his crypt constructed. But his hopes were belied, and he had to return to Changanassery. He was looked after by his relatives, and he ultimately passed away there.

I joined the school in 1996 on Sister Sinclare's recommendation. Father Kattady had his own ways of measuring a teacher's capabilities and spotting the good ones. He could judge from the amount of chalk dust on a person's hands whether he or she was a teacher of mathematics. I have been complimented by him and told that I was a good maths teacher.

Father Kattady took care to promote young male teachers too. That the school got permission to be upgraded into a senior secondary school was also because of his sole efforts. When Sister Sinclare took voluntary retirement, Sister Elsa took her place. She was a guileless and sincere nun. She carried everyone with her and ran the institution smoothly. Those were the halcyon days. Then Mathew Joseph entered the scene as the principal.

Chapter Nineteen

Even before Mathew Joseph's advent, the school had come under the complete control of the Norbertine Congregation. The noble presence and deeds of Father Kattady were obliterated, and there wasn't even a faint memory of him left in most minds. Young priests came in as school managers. Mathew Joseph had a rather short inning as the principal. The competition for the top spot in the school was heating up. Molly Joseph made her play, pushing past four of her senior colleagues. She had many aces up her sleeve to neutralize them. She was able to inveigle the priest-manager of the school very easily. She managed to get a fabricated complaint filed against the senior-most teacher to disqualify him. She had even tried to get him suspended on the pretext that he had thrown a pencil box at a student in the class. Finally, he had to go on compulsory leave.

She had curried favour with the priests managing the school to achieve all this. The priest-manager even ignored the fact that the complaint submitted against the teacher was in Molly Joseph's own handwriting. She had all of them dancing to her tune. Her aim was to ensure that the principal's job would come to her on a platter.

The events that followed were evidence that the Norbertine priests in charge were thoughtless men. They didn't condescend to listen to anyone else; they took arbitrary and unilateral decisions. They had no concern that the reputation and excellence of the school were being sacrificed.

The process of the principal's appointment was nothing less than bizarre. A male and a female teacher, who were also in the running, were long-standing and close friends. Graffiti and posters smearing these two teachers appeared on the school walls. The hearsay was that the nun who had counselled the two friends and the lady teacher ended their friendship. With Molly Joseph's machinations, they even turned enemies. The priests were mere putty in her hands.

On many occasions, I felt that the priest-managers lacked brains. They were not willing to listen to the other side. Women could easily twirl them around their little fingers. Including Molly Joseph and me, six teachers were eligible for the principal's post. The management tried to take it in writing from each of us that we were interested in the post of principal.

I decided to stay away from the rat race because I had no ambition to be the principal and, in any case, the whole process seemed rigged and not above board. And so when the school peon was dispatched to get my application, I didn't oblige them. Therefore, they finally sent it by registered post. Still I didn't respond. With three candidates in the panel recusing themselves, only three, including Molly, were left. Alex, the senior-most among them, was threatened with a suspension order and sidelined. That left Ripvan, but he was compelled to yield to the powers that be and gave up his claim.

Molly used to preside over teachers' meetings with a long face as if she was mourning the fall in the school's standards. She used to boast that she had the panacea for such ills. Not one to let go of any opportunity to gloat about her putative pedagogical and managerial capabilities, during one of the meetings she even went to the extent of offering to give up the principal's post as an ultimate sacrifice. I found her presumption and duplicitous words galling. She had assumed she would be appointed even before the formal announcement was made.

Subeesh, one of my colleagues and a priest of the Norbertine congregation himself, informed me that the decision on the principal's appointment had been taken. I decided to find out about the outcome from the priest-manager himself and called him. I suggested to him that he should pray before taking the decision and informed him with sadness how the presumptive principal had often behaved wantonly, disturbing the school's set routine and even cited examples. Molly turned coquettish in front of the priests; her feminine touch was all that it took to melt the mawkish hearts of the priests sent to manage the school.

The new priest-manager was by now eating out of her hand. The complaint given by her against me was that I wasn't teaching the students. She maligned me through her whisper campaign with some students and parents. I was summoned by the manager to his room and told that my teaching was substandard and that I ought to be more diligent in my work. After teaching more than a thousand students over two decades, I found such unsubstantiated opinions to be inconsequential and petty. I have had the gratification of turning mathematics into the favourite subject of countless students. Therefore, I decided to ignore the complaint that I knew was born out of vindictiveness and the manager's caveat. I didn't mince my words and told him that if I had been found incompetent as a teacher, I should be thrown out and not counselled.

An incident from the time when Mathew was the principal was a harbinger of what was to come. It all started with an attempt to fill the area between the high school building and the secondary school building. A number of people had lost their footing in that place and had stumbled and fallen while going from one building to the other. Ripvan Jacob advised us to put a plank of wood in that space to prevent such mishaps.

A plank of wood brought in by the students was placed there. I jumped up and down on it a couple of times to make sure it was stable and safe. However, Benny Peekkunnel, the priest in charge of construction and maintenance of the school buildings, had a different viewpoint. Ripvan was summoned to his room. Father Peekkunnel gave us a tongue-lashing in the meeting held there, as he was waiting for an opportunity to retaliate against Ripvan for some perceived slight (Ripvan had corrected him in some trivial matter). As demanded by Ripvan, the principal called for a staff meeting. I explained what had taken place.

Most of the staff were disappointed by the appointment of Molly Joseph as the principal, as successor to Joseph sir. They were worried about the decline in the school's standing. True enough, once she got power, she built a phalanx of yes-men, sycophants and rumourmongers around her. In staff meetings, she deprecated and denigrated senior teachers. Everyone grew to hate these meetings.

Chapter Twenty

A priest called Sunil Thomas took over as the manager. He spoke in a kind tone and had a soft touch. His words were full of compassion and cordiality, and everyone felt relieved. He expressed his desire to meet every staff member in person as soon as he joined. One day, after classes, as Josy—a teacher in the physics department in whose car I was commuting to school as he lived close to the convent—and I were about to leave for the convent, I got the opportunity to meet the manager. I used this chance to narrate to him what was going wrong in the school and why I thought it was headed for trouble. I held nothing back.

The principal treated senior teachers as if we were her enemies. She showed her boorishness even to teachers who were superannuating. I told him that, because of her, many of them were in tears as they left for their homes for the last time. I suggested that he should show the grace to go to their homes and console them. After listening to all that I had to say, he requested me to lend him my support.

Though I had great hopes, what transpired was just the opposite. Even he could not stay on for more than two months, given the influence Molly Joseph had and wielded ruthlessly. He was moved out.

Two and a half months later, I was stunned to receive a letter of warning alleging wrongdoings on my side. The school sports meet was on; my duty was at the hospitality centre. I was busy when the peon arrived with a six-page memo, of which I was asked to sign a copy and return to him. I said I was too preoccupied to do that and took the memo and kept it in my bag. I left after a short while through the rear entrance and reached the convent. I read the memo in my room. The charges against me were puerile and senseless. After writing out my reply, I returned to my daily routine.

One morning when I went to the office to mark my attendance with my signature, as I was reaching out for the register, I heard a bellow and saw the principal rushing towards me, screaming that I shouldn't sign it. In the register, against my name, fifteen days had been blanked out in red ink. There was a letter also suspending me from the school's services. I showed no emotion and calmly went to the staff room and read the letter. I immediately shot off a letter to the District Education Officer, the appellate authority. Missing me in class, the students came to the staff room in search of me.

The manager hadn't thought through the problems an immediate suspension order would engender. I told the truth to the students who had come to the staff room. The students asked the principal the reasons for my suspension. She ordered them out and shouted at them that it was not her handiwork. She threatened action against the students and asked them to clear off. The students of the class of which I was the class teacher decided to protest and shouted slogans against my suspension. They were caned and driven back into the classroom.

I had taken no action, nor had I instigated them. The students had composed the slogans themselves. There was a decision to convene a Parent-Teacher Association (PTA) meeting on the incident the same day. Though the parents and students were backing me, the president of the association backed out. The PTA did not agree to give permission for the students to go on strike. Though there were those who supported me, both among parents and teachers, no one had the gumption to come out in vocal support, and so they remained in the shadows.

On the second day of the complaint, the DEO came in person to investigate. Evidence was gathered from the manager, the principal and me, in that order. I gave straightforward answers to the questions he asked me. Convinced from the initial enquiry itself that there were insufficient reasons to suspend me as per the Kerala Education Act & Rules, the DEO ordered the suspension to be revoked. The order asked me to be taken back immediately. However, the management dragged their feet, and only after I was made to wait fifteen days did they take any action. I was called on the phone by the manager and asked to re-join duty.

> *Jesus said to his disciples: 'Things that cause people to stumble are bound to come, but woe to anyone through whom they come. It would be better for them to be thrown into the sea with a millstone tied around their neck than to cause one of these little ones to stumble.*
>
> Luke 17:1–2

The students welcomed me, clapping their hands and dancing and singing. Though the students wanted to meet me at the school gate and take me in a procession, 'some people' dissuaded them. I was pleasantly surprised that what I had thought was a blow to my career turned out to have such a heartening conclusion. Smiling, I wondered how I had survived the episode.

Though the antagonists of this incident had faced a backlash, they didn't remain quiet. The priest-manager and the principal continued their slander campaign against me, using a nun who was shadowing me like an avenging angel aching to see my downfall. The school management formally appealed to the Deputy Director against the DEO's stay order on my suspension. They tried to get the order rescinding my suspension withdrawn by the Education Officer by influencing the local MLA. I met the MLA in person and apprised him of the facts. He conceded that the school management had misled him. He assured me that I would have his personal and his party's support in my fight with the management. Refusing to concede anything, the management sent appeals to the Director of Public Education and to the cabinet minister.

During this time, I was offered help by a nun to attend the enquiry conducted in the Secretariat at Thiruvananthapuram. We stayed at Adhyapaka Bhavan, a hostel for teachers. The enquiry commission comprising three high-level officials took statements from the DEO, Deputy Director and Director of Public Education. At the outset itself, they pointed out that the DEO's order cannot be rescinded. They were unanimous in their opinion that a priest and nun fighting on opposing sides was disgraceful.

Chapter Twenty-One

The Provincial Superior called me and suggested that I agree to a reconciliation, and I assented. She demanded that I should withdraw my complaint. However, there was no complaint from me. What the DEO had cancelled was the suspension order served on me by the management. All the rest were appeals challenging this order, as a result of which there was little that could be done from my side.

As advised by the Provincial Superior, I decided to meet the Bishop of Mananthavady Eparchy. She accompanied me for the meeting, which was my first with him in person. From his interactions, I could understand that he had been tutored by the principal, who was also a member of the Pastoral Council, and believed her stilted version. Before I could start giving my side of the story, he stopped me, saying he was aware of everything. I became a mere listener.

His first advice was that the job I had got without paying any donation should be given up. I possessed all the qualifications to be a teacher, and I was also certain that I had won this position without any illicit actions or as a favour. I told him as much. I had sufficient qualifications and capability to be a teacher in any other school.

His second observation left me bemused. He said that if any of his flock had a difference of opinion with him on any matter, and they considered him unfit for the post of bishop, he would give up his title without batting an eyelid. The logic of this went over my head. From time to time, there had been criticism about the bishop even among the most committed faithful. A group of devotees had demanded his abdication after the rape and impregnation of a minor by Father Robin Vadakkumchery of the Mananthavady Diocese in 2016 had become a cause célèbre.

However, in that moment, I didn't feel like challenging him. Assuming that my fate was sealed, I got up deferentially from my seat. The Provincial Superior met him alone after that. I was not privy to what she filled into his ears. I was, however, certain that none of that would be in my favour.

*

I was the Deputy Examination Superintendent at the secondary examination (what in Kerala is called Secondary School Leaving Certificate or SSLC) at Kaniyaram School in Mananthavady. A squad consisting of senior officials from the examination board came to the school for inspection. One of them told me that they had received a complaint that I was not respectful towards my principal. The squad had reached us after visiting our Dwaraka school. Another member told me that the principal had tearfully unrolled a litany of complaints against me and painted me as a villain.

The rest of their recommendations revealed a soft spot for the principal. They left with bland and non-accusatory advice: it is desirable to treat the head of an institution with a little more respect. However, they also seemed to understand that personal animosity was behind the complaints and advised me that I ought to meet any attempts at slander and libel with legal action. It was a victory for me.

Many who had stood up against the steps taken by the school management and the principal retracted. That was also the fate of the complaint given by Ripvan against the principal. Due to mounting pressure from his family members and relatives, he folded up and became withdrawn.

Chapter Twenty-Two

THE SOCIAL LIFE OF NUNS IS UNDER TIGHT CONTROL. THEY LIVE WITHIN barriers. Even within the high-walled boundaries of the cloisters, they are shackled. They have very limited opportunities to move among the laity, to understand their living circumstances and intervene in their lives. The life of a nun is circumscribed in an almost literal sense by her spiritual service. Even the convents that claim to be free and have agency are entirely under the control of the paternalistic male priests. They have no right or role in policy decisions.

The mission of the sisters in the convents attached to these churches is merely to clear the path for the priests and tidy up after them. Their life experiences and the wisdom that comes with age find no value here. The attitude of the young buck priests to aged nuns is evidence of this.

The public has little knowledge of the life of nuns spent in drudgery, their faces scorched by the heat and smoke of the refectories in bishop houses and in the kitchens of monasteries. After years spent in formation and taking their perpetual vows, instead of blending themselves into the lives of the laity and doing God's ministry and spreading the gospel, Christ's brides are cursed to do the bidding of the male pastors. Until recently, nuns from the FCC had to slave away in the Mananthavady Bishop House refectory. At the most there are two or three outside helpers, but the heavy-lifting is all done by the sisters. In the Pastoral Centre in Dwaraka too, the cookhouse was run by a sister. Women who answer God's call and enter a monastic life, inspired by the prospect of living a life of service to God and humanity, end up as slaves to priests and live a life in bondage.

The parish priest has complete control over the convent. In the convent, he sits at the head of the table. The diet and recipes are for tickling his taste buds. Realizing the primacy of the male priests, nuns reconcile themselves to an unholy and immoral life of bondage. The wisdom they glean from their own life experiences is forgotten. Those sisters who do not have the strength of faith and willpower yield to the promiscuous-minded priests' desires for revelry too. They do not realize the spark of divinity in them is being snuffed out by their temporal desire to curry favour with those in power.

The inmates get news from the Provincial House and Provincial Generalate through general circulars. No one, except a chosen few, has any say in these matters. There are tall claims that the power structure in the provincial houses and convents is decided through participative and democratic methods. Victory in elections comes less through personal competence and more through the fawning pliability and readiness to seduce and humour the church elders. There is rampant groupism to build a wall of protection around themselves. They are the ones who end up as members in the Provincial Council.

Although the Church claims that even the selection of the provincial superior is a transparent process, that is far from the case. Gossiping, rumour-mongering, backbiting, lust for power—these can be found in greater measure among Christ's brides than in open society. After they have spurned riches and desires, the nuns who take the vows to follow the path of Jesus Christ in reality reach a world of power seeking and cut-throat competition.

Sometimes, women from well-to-do families and those who have a comfortable lifestyle are attracted to a monastic life primarily because of their love for God. My sister and I are examples of this. There are also those who choose the convent life due to rejection or failure of love affairs, or because of dysfunctional families. But the majority of them are seen off by their families unwillingly and with heavy hearts. Often, they have to forfeit a sizeable inheritance to join the convent. The forfeiture of all inheritance has to be given in writing. The rules of the FCC stipulate that one has to start from a zero bank account, but this mainly applies to those who receive their salaries from the government. The others have no bank accounts of their own.

The Church uses different strategies for evangelism. The main among them is snaring aspirants for the monastic and priestly trade. In this long-term strategy, temporal and spiritual matters are intertwined inseparably. The primary responsibility is to lead the students in schools and catechism classes towards devoutness. In the convents, province counsellors take the lead for this. A cadre called 'vocation promoters' is also deployed towards this end.

The system works by collecting telephone numbers from the children who attend camps organized by the Church and getting in touch with their parents. This continues until they reach Class 10. Then the children are indoctrinated on the benefits of choosing a monastic life. The families are also advised to use such opportunities to overcome poverty. This will never be mentioned in an open forum. This will be done by buttonholing individuals or by penetrating into families. Potential candidates and their influencers are attracted by small financial loans. The children who are inmates of Balabhavan are also used for evangelism and in God's service. Children are prepared for ministry and evangelism through indoctrination.

Priests and nuns will descend on Church-run schools at the start of the academic year itself to do ministry work. The principals' and headmistresses' responsibility is to set the stage for them. One of the prerequisites for such posts is this capability. In the Sacred Heart School in Dwaraka, announcements used to be made that Christian children should meet these evangelists during the lunch break.

This activity went by the name of 'catch them young'. The different orders used to compete among themselves to see how many children each of them could snatch. They were willing to go to any lengths to succeed. The unrelenting counselling they are subjected to wipes out independent thought in the children. Their yearning to undertake a spiritual mission will be misinterpreted and limited to the phrase 'God's call'. This is a catchphrase of Kerala Christians. In reality, it is the echo of one's conscience that comes from within. A compelling impetus to do good, which, interpreted narrowly and misinterpreted as God's call, becomes a mission to ferry novices to seminaries and convents.

Chapter Twenty-Three

I FELT MORTIFIED THAT I COULDN'T HELP THE AFOREMENTIONED FRIEND'S family with the ten thousand rupees that they needed. A bigger humiliation was that the authorities wouldn't even give me a rejection letter. When I had expressed the desire to publish my poems and other prose works, and cut a CD of the hymns that I had composed, I was met with the same stony silence. When I sought permission to take a driving licence, they stonewalled me.

I have referred to the Consecrated Life course conducted by Father James Kannanthanam that I had attended to get over the turmoil in my life at one point in time. I had always treated him with respect. I had him read some of my creations and he encouraged me to continue writing. Though we had a mental affinity, I used to call him only once in a year or so. Once when he had visited Mananthavady Provincial House, I had shown him my entire corpus of literary creations and won his approbation.

When I chanced upon a music teacher with whom I could get along well, my desire to cut the CD was rekindled. When I made a request to the office of the Provincial Superior, on this and publishing my works, they turned mute. It is not as though I had asked permission verbally; I had submitted a proper written request. While I was fighting these battles on one front, on the other, I got involved in all the activities in the school. I led the way in the collection of funds for my co-workers who were not receiving their salaries due to various legal tangles they were caught in. I was also a member of the group who, on finding the penurious state of the family of one of our students, set out to get a house built for them.

The convent and the Church started to misconstrue my liberated lifestyle as insubordination. I was, however, determined to not surrender my freedom at any cost. Though I had no explicit permission, I cut the CD of Christian hymns written by me. About three hundred people graced the CD release event in a hall in Peechamkode, near Mananthavady; the CD was released by Spadikam George, a well-known cine actor and evangelist. Only five nuns, including me, were present, and of those only three were from my congregation. I had invited the Provincial Superior, Sister Stephina, to give the felicitation speech and had printed her name on the flyers, but she didn't turn up. This was chalked up as another charge against me later—that I had included her name in the flyer without permission.

Nuns have released music CDs not only in Mananthavady but also in many other provinces. They have written and published books too. The respective provincial houses take over the entire responsibility for printing and publishing. Considering that I was a teacher for over twenty years and was drawing my salary from the government, what the authorities did to me was iniquitous because I have never failed to entrust my salary to the convent, in accordance with the stipulation.

Not only did they not show any consideration for my aspirations, but they also rebuffed me completely. My lyrics were set to music by leading composers. The orchestra consisted of talented musicians. The vocals were handled by recognized singers. I even managed to include promising local youngsters. But neither the Church nor the convent inmates helped me in any way. My well-wishers from outside the convent, however, supported me all through.

The desire to have my poems and essays brought out in book form suffered a similar fate with the Church hierarchy. I took the decision to self-publish, considering it to be God's will. I entered into a contract with a Kozhikode-based publisher. The collection of poems titled *Snehamazhayil* (In Showers of Love) is still lying around unsold. The Church didn't take any steps to distribute it, even among children.

I have already touched upon their inaction, which went on for over a year, in relation to my request to be permitted to learn driving. There was no ban on nuns learning to drive. However, the Mananthavady Province had decided not to buy a vehicle for itself. At the same time, I never felt that by not obeying the order of the Church authorities or choosing not to honour their requests, I was breaching the vow of obedience as a nun.

A desire that I should prove I am an independent-minded woman had risen within me. As long as I thought it was morally right, the urge to do it was an inborn trait in me, especially if someone asked me not to do it. If someone asked me not to say something, I couldn't stop myself from saying it out loud. Perhaps this foible of mine is what brought things to a head in this fashion.

I joined the St. Mary's Driving School in a locality called Anjukunnu. My instructor was Susie Thomas, one of our parishioners. I had informed my mother of my desire to learn driving and had sought her permission. She instead reminded me of an old incident and told me this should not be a repeat of that one.

The incident she was referring to had taken place during my stay in Hassan for my BEd course. We had a fortnight's holiday. The then Provincial Superior of Mananthavady was also with me. After we had joined the convent, most of our education courses happened concurrently. We were very close and were fond of each other.

Since I had completed my lessons already, I set off on a bicycle to fetch a book for a friend from another girl staying outside the convent. A milkman was riding ahead of me with milk cans suspended on either side of his cycle. Since I was pedalling rather fast, I kept ringing the bell, hoping he would give way. However, he rode on, ignoring me. It was a busy road. I was unable to control the cycle and crashed into the milkman, even as cars and other vehicles whizzed past us.

He and his cycle went down in a heap. My leg was hurt. I picked up the veil that had flown off my head. The milk was flowing down the road. The milkman started to shout, demanding compensation. Some college students at a nearby teashop came to my aid, probably feeling some sympathy for me. I told the milkman that if he was prepared to go with me to the pastor of the church, I would get him the money. I was no longer able to ride the cycle. I pushed it all along the national highway, despite the blood oozing out of my leg. As soon as I could, I dumped the cycle in the courtyard of one of my acquaintances who lived nearby and then went to the convent.

Such mishaps never make me nervous. My style is to face adversity boldly.

Chapter Twenty-Four

Notwithstanding the displeasure and opposition of the convent superiors, I completed my driving course and earned my licence. Next came the desire to buy a car. There was a ban on owning personal vehicles, so I had to struggle to overcome that proscription. Even though such bans existed, most of our journeys were made using private vehicles. There was no interdiction against travelling with priests in their cars. I, however, was not in favour of this. I thought that if the nuns who had no occupation of their own could be taught driving and given cars, the transportation problem of convent inmates could be solved easily. I had even placed this suggestion before the authorities.

One of the sisters in Mananthavady Province had been using a two-wheeler for a long time. I realized that those favoured by the authorities received such extraordinary dispensations. I decided to take the pig-headedness of the authorities head-on, and so I dealt with them summarily. As an independent-minded woman, I had decided to break free of their restrictions. I bought a car and, thereafter, all my travels were in it. Not a single nun was ready to travel in it. But my students used to wait for me. Truly, it became a children's car.

None of the sisters who had goaded me to learn driving backed me at this juncture. When they used to motivate me, I had no interest in driving. Unwarranted and irrational opposition to and denial of my desires and ideas provokes and impels me to do things. I decided to show them my mettle through my actions. When I decided to buy a car, the question of where it would be parked arose. Mother Superior said that it shouldn't be parked inside the convent. My stand was this: let the car come first, then we shall see.

The realization that the ability to drive a car boosts a woman's self-esteem came to me late in life. I am reminded of something at this point. Sister Celine Vazhackal from my batch of nuns had studied only till Class 10. I used to call her Vazhakunju (*kunju* meaning baby or child). The Christian community sets great store by education; educational qualifications are considered great achievements. Yet, I have always felt that convents were also not free from discrimination based on education. Since this discrimination was practised in the open, the less-educated sisters used to suffer from considerable inferiority complex.

Celine used to be fond of cows. The convent's superiors realized this and encouraged her to take care of the cattle. She was always engaged in cutting grass for the cows, milking them, washing them and the like. Under her care, the cows started to give more milk than was consumed within the convent. During this time, she came to own a mobile phone, but when she asked for fifty rupees to recharge it, Mother Superior refused to give her the sum. Although she used to spend liberally on her own travel and personal needs, she chose to deny Celine a paltry fifty rupees. She gave in only when the murmurs and appeals became strident and couldn't be ignored.

*

My mother was ill once, but I only came to know of it when I went home during the holidays. I had then accompanied her to the hospital and was her caregiver for some time. I have suffered on many occasions on account of not having a personal phone. If the call came to the convent, the fellow nuns would often give the excuse that it was prayer time in order to not have to call me to the phone. On other occasions, my ongoing conversation was interrupted.

Realizing what I was going through, my mother asked my brother to buy me a mobile phone. Before we left the hospital, I had, with the help of some people, learnt how to use it. Though it was not the general dispensation in the convent, I decided to use the phone.

People who are not smart and cannot stand up for themselves tend to get discounted. One of my colleagues, Sister Philcy, is an example. She owned no mobile phone, due to which I had seen her struggle when she was the locum for the principal. I found this humiliating. She used to borrow phones from other teachers when she had to use one during emergencies.

Though the authorities were not unaware of this, they made no move to buy her a phone. Finally, I prepared and submitted an application on her behalf. The authorities sanctioned only a paltry two thousand rupees for the phone and that too grudgingly. I taught her how to use the phone.

An incident at Kommayad convent when both of us were inmates is relevant here. We were in the midst of planning a one-day excursion trip for catechism teachers. Philcy informed the group that, due to indifferent health, she would have to give the trip a miss. The priest in charge flew into a rage. He announced that if she was not taking the trip, she need not take catechism classes any more.

Contrary to my understanding of her and in a tone uncharacteristic of her, given her peaceable nature, she retorted with equal vehemence, 'If that's the case, I have no desire to do it. I have been giving catechism classes for thirty years. If it is not there, it is not there. I am not running after it.' A distressed Philcy informed the Provincial Superior. Stephina's response was to ask her why she had responded in that fashion. And she was told that she should have cooperated with him at any cost. This was shocking, aware as Stephina was that Philcy was under medication. Despite her ailment, she had to finally go on the trip. This is just one instance of the subjugation we as women had to undergo, not only at the hands of those in positions of authority but also the priests.

Another matter of note is that the physicality of a woman will reflect in and affect her mind and actions. Those who work outside the convent, including people like me, have had to face these inconveniences. The nuns do not even have the freedom to choose the type of sanitary napkins during their monthly periods. They are forced to use pads that have poor absorption qualities. My request to the Provincial Superior to buy better-quality—and therefore higher-priced—pads was turned down. Her rationalization was that though she was travelling more than me, her own pads were of poorer quality.

Even the use of sanitary pads was started pretty recently in convents. New entrants were usually given a roll of white cloth. This was used during menstruation over time. Things have improved in convents now. It is heartening that the new generation of nuns shows the forthrightness to buy and use better-quality sanitary napkins.

Although nuns are given allowances for use in emergencies in the convents of some congregations, FCC didn't have this practice. The allowance was given to the nuns to provide for exigencies such as menstruation, but we had to beg the authorities to actually use it. Our clothing was also decided based on an annual survey. We had to plead for undergarments. Undergarments from close-down sales of resellers or warehouse sales of manufacturers were collected in the Provincial House. The preferences of actual users were neither asked for nor listened to. The only option was to pick what was available, whether it fitted or not.

I couldn't stomach some of the ways of the convent. One of the main ones was the gossip session that took place at the dining table. The male priests would lead the way with slander about parishioners and nuns who were not present. In any case, the priest was at the head of the table.

One piece of gossip that used to go around while I was at Kavumannam is a good example. A Class 5 student of catechism was the target. Not merely were his own failings bruited about, even his parents and grandparents were subjected to character assassination. The nuns encouraged the vicar, adding fuel to the fire.

It all started with the small child being scolded and detained in the chapel by the vicar for not bringing a pen or possibly running back to his home to get one as he had forgotten to bring it to the catechism class. For this minor transgression, which should have been smiled at, for over an hour the priest had berated him and his entire lineage was called into question, and derogatory language was used.

The child's mother eventually arrived on the scene. Being a spirited woman, she took umbrage at the mental torture her poor son was put through. The priest made the mistake of calling her character into question and even used words such as slut or worse. She tried to slap the priest, and the commotion caught the attention of the other people running the classes, including me. Since the priest knew he would find no support or sympathy from me, he turned on me and said that I should mind my own business and stick to my work in the high school as this was a middle-school matter and there were other people to look into it. Then the vilification campaign started. Hurt by all the gratuitous calumny, the family withdrew the child from the catechism classes.

The convent welcomed different guests differently, which too did not sit well with me. The poor were met outside the gates; others in the parlour. Nuns who were happy to spend hours at a time in the company of visiting priests would show much reluctance to meet the poor supplicants. Their demeanour would make it clear, to the poor at least, that they should finish their business and leave quickly. Those whom they favoured could go beyond the walls and more.

> *For if a man with a gold ring, in fine clothing, comes into your assembly, and also a poor man in ragged clothing comes in, and you have respect for him who wears the fine clothing and say to him, 'Sit here in a good place,' and say to the poor, 'Stand there,' or 'Sit here under my footstool,' have you not then become partial among yourselves and become judges with evil thoughts?*
>
> James 2:2–4

The words of Apostle James have been among the main revelations of my monastic life. I had no doubt about how the rich and the poor should be treated.

Chapter Twenty-Five

THE PROVINCIAL HOUSE, IN THE MEANTIME, HAD HONED THEIR KNIVES and fine-tuned their strategies to crucify me. The CD release, my book of poems, the driving licence, the car and suspension by the school—all became grist to the mill. The Provincial Superior's warning letter contained the threat that I would be rendered an outcast in my order. I was not worried in the least. For me, life was not to be spent fretting. I had decided that I would stay rational and live a happy life. Not only did I not bother to respond to the letter, I didn't even consider it to be of any import.

The Provincial Superior Sister Stephina, along with Sister Jyothi Maria, came to the convent to meet me. They said that they needed me to make some decisions. They told me with considerable arrogance that I couldn't carry on in the fashion I had been. I asked them for explanations in relation to each of the charges laid out in the letter. I showed them no disrespect or distrust. Their visit had a definite objective: to browbeat me and subdue me. They probably thought that I would confess, burst into tears and ask for their forgiveness. Even the bishop, the congregation and other members of the order must have thought likewise. But I stuck to my guns; I was not ready to become a serf. I decided to continue the fight.

The 'Save Our Sister' campaign, run by the nuns from the beginning of September 2018, culminated in Bishop Franco's arrest on 20 September 2018. The judicial moves against him started the day after my visit to the protest pandal. As evidenced by various news reports, the Church put its considerable heft behind him. I felt gratified that I was able to uphold the monastic vows of being on the side of the oppressed and the meek. I was relieved that I was able to join the sisters who had sacrificed much to bring out their struggle onto the streets to get justice. As much as the Church tried to distance me from the flock through its hierarchy, I moved closer to them by getting involved in everything that was happening in the parish.

I was quite taken up with the idea of the Women's Wall organized by the Kerala government on 1 January 2019 to strengthen women's empowerment following the imbroglio related to the entry of women into the Sabarimala temple. On the same day, clad in a churidar-kameez set, I posted a photo of myself on Facebook, felicitating the Women's Wall. This annoyed the authorities even more and their opposition to me became stronger.

From the very beginning, I had definite views on nuns' habits, which I thought needed drastic redesigning. The habit that covers nuns from head to toe has caused health issues. The polyester fabric often used is most unsuitable in torrid zones. Especially in Kerala, with its unvarying climate, the habit is insufferable. Its design should change with the times and climes.

I am not able to tolerate a warm climate; I have always preferred cool weather, and my heart yearns for cooler temperatures. During the hot summers, my body, swathed in the head-to-toe habit, would be drenched in sweat. The dresses of nuns in other countries and even in other states of India have undergone changes. They have succeeded in selecting attire suitable to their climate. Nuns should have the freedom to choose Indian traditional dresses such as sarees and salwar-kameezes.

Many congregations outside Kerala, and of late inside the state, too, have given their nuns some latitude in relation to the choice of clothes. The same Code of Canons applies to all brothers and sisters who have chosen to lead a monastic life, except ordained male priests. And except for nuns, the others are exempt in many matters. For instance, the others have the right to wear the attire they desire. Not only in clothing, they also have no restrictions pertaining to the use of vehicles and recreation. The truth is that the restrictions are not intrinsic to the system.

However, the Church is not willing to give women a fraction of the consideration that society at large gives its male members. The clergy—who have thrown off such restrictions on ordained priesthood and monasticism—aren't in the least ready to accept even minor advancements made by nuns.

In Kerala, a few congregations have taken on board these changes. In a way, the regimental habit is a strategy for continuing the enslavement of nuns. For society, the characteristics and personality of a nun do not constitute the spiritual energy she has gained over many years through her life full of sacrifices. The manifestation is a raiment that swaddles her person entirely.

The habit plays a major role in denying nuns a liberated life shorn of the shackles of monasticism. Once a woman has been a nun, society will not accept her as a layperson. In reality, every nun is a slave when inside the habit. These are not random thoughts flitting through my mind but well-thought-out positions based on experience. Likewise, my decision to wear a churidar-kameez set was thought through and decided upon using cold logic.

The parish at Karimbil, a hamlet near Mananthavady, was a small one with very few members. Sister Vinaya was a member of the Clarist congregation in this parish and lived in the convent. She had a cordial relationship with all the families of the parish. The torture she went through after she went to watch a movie with one of the parish families can be ascribed to the habit. When she emerged out of the theatre after the movie, a brother from CST Dwaraka saw her. Notwithstanding that he too had watched the same movie, he called the Provincial Superior at Mananthavady and reported her outing. Early the next morning, the authorities arrived in a car and took her to Prarthana Bhavan (prayer house) in Dwaraka. She was virtually a prisoner there for many months, where she was being punished for her transgression, ostensibly in penitential prayers.

My social media posts and frank opinions found a place in the list of charges against me. The desire of the orthodoxy within the Church to ostracize and isolate me completely took a new turn. I left the prayer group in the convent. My heart didn't allow me to join those who had ostracized me even in prayer. However, I was not going to give up my own prayers and used to pray to Jesus Christ on my own and at my convenience.

Chapter Twenty-Six

A NUN'S LIFE IS FULL OF STRIFE. AFTER SHE SETS OUT ON HER MONASTIC life with unbounded love for Jesus Christ, she has to countenance a life of slavery in a way. Independent thinking and emotions are made out to be alien to them. And they are alienated from such human qualities by diktats. Those who do not willingly submit to servitude are put under severe mental stress. The term enslavement is very true in the case of nuns.

One of the ways to calm the storm that rages inside a nun, or anyone leading a monastic life, is meditation. Many years ago, to discover and attain beatitude, all the nuns in the Church were made to attend a forty-day silent retreat. Retreats have a special place in nuns' lives. The belief is that they not only assuage their mental tensions but would elevate them to a high level of spirituality. Meditation is also aimed at helping them continually overcome the trauma of forsaking a worldly life.

I believe that the determination I have developed is a reflection of the spiritual energy I had received from that retreat, in which I was also a participant. As it was a silent retreat, we were not allowed to talk to one another. All conversations were to be held with God alone.

I wondered how roommates were able to abide by the instructions to maintain silence even between themselves.

One night I was woken up by sounds coming from a bed next to mine. I realized someone was singing 'Happy Birthday to You'. I asked how such things were permitted when even conversation was banned. In response, I got a sweet, innocent answer from the nun in question: she was only wishing the vicar. This was one moment when I felt that silent retreats were turning into mere pretence. I realized that each nun was fully involved in her individual life, and this incident taught me that unless they were willing to struggle and work hard, they would not be able to free themselves from these entanglements.

Another incident around the same time reinforced my observations. The loud snoring of a nun from a nearby bed was disturbing my sleep; unable to bear it much longer, I decided to wake her up. I shook her saying '*koorkkam, koorkkam*', which is the vernacular for snore. In her sleep, she heard it as '*moorkhan, moorkhan*', cobra. She leapt out of the bed with screams of 'cobra'; it took us a long time to calm her down. It made me wonder how many of us had really found serenity through retreats and meditation.

Once, at our retreat centre, I witnessed an old man being denied a response to his question by a senior nun. On her part, she was only observing the rule of the silent retreat. However, unsure how right or righteous it was to have done this, I went up to the man and asked him what it was that he was seeking to find an answer to. He told me that he had come to the retreat centre in search of a certain clergyman. I took him to the priest he was looking for. The righteous thing to do at that point was to help the man. The few words that I had to utter to do this had not affected the observance of the silent retreat, in my view.

Chapter Twenty-Seven

Once a journalist friend came to meet me at the convent. She reached our convent late, as there was a traffic jam on the way. It was not safe for her to return alone in the night after meeting me. Our attempts to find a place for her to stay outside didn't meet with success. So I introduced her to Mother Superior as my relative. The rice left over from our lunch, with water added to it (a common practice to prevent it from being spoiled), was available in the refectory. We both had that unpalatable repast for dinner. We then found that the guest room was locked. Sensing the resentment of the convent inmates, the unnerved visitor told me piteously that she wasn't keen on a room for herself.

So I asked her to come to my room. I took a bedsheet from one of the cupboards and spread it on the floor next to my bed. It was so uncomfortable that she was not able to sleep the whole night. Only the next morning, after I had left for Holy Mass, was she finally able to sleep on my bed to get over her tiredness. The convent authorities chose to wilfully misinterpret her arrival and presence. Some of the inmates had become a conduit for information to the higher echelons and had reported the presence of my guest to the higher-ups—albeit with a twist. I was certain that the doubts that were subsequently raised about whether it was a man who had slept in my room were the handiwork of such malicious communicators.

*

All my replies to the letters and notices I received from the FCC Generalate and Provincial House were prepared by me personally. Later, I thought that I should take the help of a lawyer. As a last resort, I sent the authorities an open letter. But they had already taken a decision to expel me from the order. Their verdict made no difference to me.

My work as a teacher continued without many disruptions. Though the principal still held a grudge against me, she didn't do anything provocative. I informed the convent of my wish to attend a retreat in Vagamon. The approval came with instructions to record my experiences on paper. The peaceful atmosphere and scenic beauty of Vagamon—a hill station spread over Kottayam and Idukki districts and located about 350 km from Mananthavady—had a calming influence on me. On Maundy Thursday, we all went to the church on the high hilltop near the evocatively called Kurishumala, which means crucifix hill, to partake of the Pesaha appam, the unleavened Passover bread. The FCC convent at Vagamon was established by a nun who had gone there in her search for truth and had stayed on all by herself. In her venerable company, our stay was very pleasant. The foot-washing ceremony, part of the Maundy Thursday service, was led by a nun from our group. I experienced spiritual ecstasy from communing with nature there.

After the retreat, when I returned to my convent, I was amazed. All the six previous inmates had been transferred and had even moved out. A new group of four nuns was there. They were unwilling to talk to me. I was perplexed and felt scared. I was sure that I would have to face terrifying circumstances. I called a few people for succour. I felt that I couldn't live there for any length of time.

Perhaps it was God's mercy towards me that put paid to thoughts of moving out of the convent. I calmed down; after I regained my courage, the way forward became clear to me.

When I went to the kitchen, the cook was missing. She had been dismissed. The TV in the dining room had been powered down. The front door of the convent was locked. Though none of this escaped my attention, I was not going to be shaken. Instead, I decided to join them at the dining table and break bread with them.

One night, with a view to getting close to them, I went to the dining hall. Taking a plate from the cupboard, I sat across from Mother Superior. I kept trying to make conversation with her; all I received in response were grunts and ho-hums. I could sense that nervousness was creeping into the enemy ranks. I decided to exploit it to the hilt. Even when there was no response, I kept up my side of the conversation. I believed I had triumphed over one more adversity.

I desired to talk to them more openly. At the next mealtime, I decided I would talk at greater length. However, to do so, I was forced to wait for a few days more as they did their best to keep avoiding me. When the opportunity arose, I asked them point-blank why they were treating me as an adversary and trying to ostracize me.

The leader of the pack, Mother Superior Ligi Maria, spoke on behalf of all of them. 'You don't even know Bishop Mar Jose Porunnedom (the Bishop of Manathavady Diocese) well enough. How, then, can you know about Bishop Franco, who is so far away from you? How can you see him as an offender when you know so little about him?'

'Is there anyone in this group who has not been caressed and touched by priests? When you have been similarly molested, how can you now not have empathy for the sisters in Jalandhar?' I asked.

Unable to counter me, they all remained silent. Marina, who was in charge of mentoring novices, was the eldest nun of the lot. I narrated to her the lewd messages sent to a priest by one of the nuns trained by her. The messages were sent by mistake to another mobile number. That was how I had come to hear of them. I asked her, 'Is this the mentoring that you do? We nuns have been exploited by the priests all the time. Knowing this well, shouldn't we stand united as one and fight the injustice? The agitation at Vanchi Square by Save Our Sisters was an opportunity given to us on a platter. Didn't we waste that too?'

Ligi Maria had nothing to say.

*

Breakfast at the convent used to be at 8 a.m. Lunch was with students in the school. I used to eat a portion of what was prepared for the schoolchildren. With my ostracism, my routine underwent a change. Since the cook had been dismissed, food was cooked by the inmates. However, except me, no one else showed any alacrity. One had to go hungry for hours together. Since I had to report at the school on time, on many occasions I had to forgo my breakfast. I had to eat what my colleagues, including the nuns, shared with me to quell my hunger. Realizing their inconvenience, I started to break my fast with snacks from one of the small teashops near the convent at Karakkamala before going to the school.

I continued as if nothing had happened and kept myself preoccupied. I was removed from catechism classes, family ward prayers and conducting services; the responsibilities were given to another group. The main duty of the novices on home visits as part of their evangelical duties became to spread propaganda against me. They went about exhorting parishioners to cut all ties with me as I was 'indulging in anti-Church activities'. The aim of the propaganda spread by the authorities through these nuns was not limited to my ostracism; they wanted my excommunication. Vicar Stephen Kottakkal helmed all these initiatives. I was not allowed to be present at any wedding in the parish, house visits, house-warming events and last sacraments. However, I used to reach the dead person's house whenever I found out about the demise; invariably, I would find out only because of the death knell that was sounded at the church.

The new group was sent on a mission of smoking me out of the convent. The authorities had handpicked the hatchet women capable of this. Ligi Maria was made the Mother Superior to this end. I came to know that the group had, before they came and took charge at the convent, given their word to Provincial Superior that they would have me thrown out.

Usually, all of us would leave and return through the rear door to attend the service in the church. The priests also used to come to the convent through this door for their meals. Since the front door was usually locked, this became the only ingress and egress. With the cook leaving, this door also came under lock and key.

Ligi and her henchwomen ensured I was not a participant in communal prayers, fasting, prayers during the circumambulation of the convent, the Way of the Cross and praying the rosary. On many days, when I went for my breakfast, I was met by empty plates. When I asked them if they weren't eating, their reply was that they were fasting for a month. When I told them they should have told me earlier so I would have at least bought rice dumplings on my way back from the school, they looked stunned. When they realized that each of their well-thought-out strategies was not quelling me, they thought up more tactics and waited for opportunities to use them. I went about boldly as if none of them was affecting me.

One day, as I sat in my room, Ligi Maria sent someone and asked me to go downstairs to meet her. When I went downstairs, I saw Provincial Superior General Jyothi Maria and a Provisional

Councillor sitting with her. They were carrying two orders—the first one expelled me from the convent; the other was a collation of documents that gave the reasons for my ejection. Thrusting both at me, Jyothi Maria asked me to sign a copy as an acknowledgement.

As I started to read the expulsion order, she instructed me to sign the copy and give it back first as they were in a hurry to leave. I simply told her not to harass me in this manner. I slowly went up to my room and bolted the door behind me. I read the expulsion order and signed the copy. Before I could read the rest, Ligi Maria came and knocked at my door. However, I had decided that I wouldn't sign the dismissal decree without reading it first, though they all insisted, with Jyothi Maria stating she was only carrying out her responsibility as the Provincial Superior; I was not swayed by their pitch.

*

At that time, I had started to get headaches frequently. One evening when I went down to the dining room to get some hot water for relief, I found Mother Superior standing guard at the door of the convent. I ignored her, went to the kitchen, boiled some tea and drank it. Then I went back to my room and slept.

I realized that Ligi's aim was to lock me out of the convent as soon as I went out for mass. I didn't fall into the trap and foiled her plan by not going to church. Mother Superior also couldn't attend mass as she was waiting at the door. This went on for two days.

On the third day, when I went to the door, I found it locked from outside. The front door was anyway already locked permanently. I knew I had been tricked and registered a complaint with the police. I made them aware that a pre-written script was being followed. Though the police came and got the door opened, the convent fixed three more CCTV cameras in the kitchen, refectory and corridor. I told Ligi Maria and her flunkeys that there should have been advance notice before fixing the cameras. Their glib reply was that they tried to, but I was unreachable. In between, something else happened. The perpetrators had the police's ears and became friendly with the policemen who came to conduct the enquiry.

I then saw that the front door was being locked from the inside. I went there and asked them not to do it. Though at first they insisted that the door would remain closed, eventually they had to give in. I managed to get hold of the key and refused to give it back. They showed no consideration towards the outsider who was a resident in the convent. The next day, they used a new lock on the door. Every nun's room was locked in a similar manner. I hung the by now useless key in front of the Mother Superior's room for all to see. I saluted at the camera in the corridor in front of her room.

Fourteen CCTV cameras were fixed at various places—at every door, in the dining room, corridors, facing every room, refectory, kitchen … why, even facing my room and the toilet I used. I treated them as jokes and used to talk to the cameras for a lark. After being isolated and removed from every conversation, it was a relief for me to talk to and make gestures at the camera lenses. The nuns had become so abjectly servile that they couldn't even recognize the cameras as an invasion of their own privacy.

Chapter Twenty-Eight

When I went home for the Onam vacation, my mother asked me not to go back to the convent. She suggested that I take a house on rent in Mananthavady and continue to serve as a teacher. She also suggested that I adopt two orphan girls and become their refuge. I saw the fear in her eyes—*they will finish you*, my mother warned me. I was not ready to abide by what she said. She even went to the extent of telling me I should avoid eating from the convent. She feared I would be poisoned and killed.

The isolation and negativity that I suffered at the hands of the nuns in the convent had strengthened my determination and courage. In the normal course of things, no one would have been able to countenance the cruel betrayal shown by the Church hierarchy after one had served as God's maid all of one's adult life. I thought I should heed my mother's warning about having convent food. There was one more reason to stop eating in the convent. I can still recall the look of aversion and repugnance on my dining tablemates' faces during the days I spent there as a hated and reviled person. Even those who washed the dishes of the others ignored me completely. I felt that my mother's misgivings were not out of place.

From the next day, I started to have food separately. Other than food from the school, I mainly used to consume fruits. I did this for about ten days but grew tired of the fare. I peeped into the kitchen and saw chicken curry bubbling away on the stove. I was famished. I went to the post office and sent off some registered letters. When I got back, I could see steaming hot rice, chicken curry and sautéed vegetable with grated coconut on the dining table. I took a plate from the cupboard and had my fill of everything. After that, I washed the dish I had used and stashed it away in a secret place. I let out a burp of satisfaction and didn't forget to wink at the camera to record my gratitude.

On another occasion, I found out that they had kept a separate plate only for me. They had taken away the plate I used to eat in before this. I discovered that I was an untouchable from the snippet of a conversation I overheard during dinner that day. Someone had sarcastically asked whether I had left with my plate. Though it didn't bother me much at that time, I realized its import only later. Anyway, at that time, I let her go with a snappy retort: 'Doesn't a look at your camera tell you the tale?'

Their efforts to smoke me out continued. They pushed me to the limits of my suffering by not repairing the TV, not getting a refill for the LPG cylinder and even disconnecting the power supply. They bought an induction cooker for their cooking. Though they showed their displeasure, I used it to boil water and for other essential heating. Eventually, they disconnected the electricity supply to my room. When I returned from school and discovered the mischief, I asked in a loud voice if Mother Superior was around. That was enough for the connection to be restored.

Chapter Twenty-Nine

I REALIZED THAT THE MONASTIC LIFE OF MY DREAMS WAS BEING disrupted. It was my belief that the Church needed another Reformation. Though sometimes it seemed to be taking progressive steps, it frequently retreated before reaching the destination. My experience has shown me that instead of achieving their life's mission of serving the poor, the nuns were being suffocated and their lives were rotting away within the walls of the convent. For instance, my efforts to help a parishioner, Baby Parunthumplakkal—sickly and leading a life of misery and rejected by everyone—came to nought because of this attitude of the authorities. I was not able to visit the home of a youth who had committed suicide and console his family. Neither the high priests nor the apostolic evangelists could answer the doubts that used to crop up in my mind from time to time. Many such unanswered questions were floating in the wind. What kept me going was the irrepressible enthusiasm created by my high sense of duty and solicitude for carrying out my duty to God. The righteousness and sense of equity that I had inherited had made me capable of this.

Our genes had made the Kalapurakkal family—of which my grandfather, father and I were scions—stand out among the denizens of our region. The family's lifestyle hewed close to the gospel of Jesus Christ. During our childhood, we never experienced or practised anything immoral. While the family atmosphere was one of godliness, none of us were zealots. Church on Sundays was the only practice that was insisted upon. None of us was compelled to attend catechism classes. Fasting as a ritual was confined to Good Friday. There was an expansive liberal outlook in all of us.

Memories of my first communion, a landmark in a Christian's life, are fresh in my mind. Once the date was decided, I was all agog; I couldn't even sleep for a few nights. I waited for the grace of the angel that would appear once I accepted my first communion. My sisters had started decking me up from the previous day itself. Collecting flowers from around the house, they made a crown of flowers and bouquets. I wore pure white clothes. I was a short girl; I remember the photographer who had come to cover the ceremony lifting me up and placing me on a seat.

There is a tradition of making one's confession ahead of the First Holy Communion. I first heard of the sacrament of confession in the catechism class. The confessional is from where blessings follow. The confession is heard by the representative of Jesus Christ. Absolution from one's sins is what should happen there. The First Holy Communion usually takes place when one is eight or nine years old. The sins committed—whether advertently or inadvertently—are confessed to God's representative and exculpation is requested. Immature and ingenuous children see this as a mere ritual. They recite trivialities such as 'I stole a pencil', 'I pinched my friend', 'I lied' and so on. They then submit that they won't repeat these mistakes and ask for forgiveness.

*

Elamma, my older sister, was a nun for almost twenty-five years and had led a spiritually inspired life, but she finally left it and entered domesticity. Her decision to quit the monastic life was not instigated by any outside agency. As soon as she had completed her tenth class, she had started her campaign to join the convent. An indifferent student, she had no interest in further studies; she wanted to lead a quiet life.

Generally, the impetus to take the vows begins to form in girls from their participation in various church programmes during the holidays. The greatness of a monastic life dedicated to God and the Church is drummed up by the evangelists. They will present it as a way to overcome the daily challenges in life. Some girls are drawn by a vision that it is God's call and take up the path. This opportunity is evaluated differently by those coming from diverse backgrounds. Those from poor families will see this as a way to escape poverty. However, neither Elamma nor I suffered any privations in our life.

The whole family had stood as one against Elamma's wishes to join the convent. Kunjaanjaa stated categorically she wasn't going anywhere. In an effort to dissuade her, she was admitted to the non-regular college he had started by then. Though she was railroaded into joining the pre-degree course, she resisted and dug in her heels. She locked herself up and went on a fast. All the efforts of the family came to nought in front of her uncompromising obduracy. They finally gave in to her wishes.

After three years of formation, she joined Nirmalagiri College for her pre-degree course. I was already there doing my second year of graduation. Her taking the vows was a happy occasion. However, she had joined the college unable to withstand the immense pressure from the convent authorities. She barely managed to squeak through the pre-degree examination and showed no inclination to pursue an undergraduate course. The convent decided to make her join a lab technician training course. She tried to get out of that citing her ignorance of the English language.

Though she did resist the decision, she was compelled to join the course. After completing the course, she was appointed in a hospital run by the Church. She chafed at the lab technician's job, as she wanted a life of ease. She conveyed her apathy openly to both Chachan and Kunjaanjaa.

At that time, she met with an accident when the vehicle she was travelling in overturned, and she injured her spine. So bad was her condition that she was bedridden for almost six months in the Provincial House at Malaparamba. Once she recovered, she put her foot down and said she was not going to resume duty in the hospital. Without heeding her preference for a quiet life, the convent authorities made her join a pre-primary teachers' course in Bangalore and after its completion appointed her as a teacher in an English-medium school in Perambra run by the FCC Thamarassery Province. Her life dragged on between the convent at Kodencheri, where she was put up and where she worked in a school.

Eventually, she was fed up with the petty rivalries between convents and the squabbles between the inmates. She was repulsed by the sight of the clergymen and nuns clawing at one another. When she had to witness incidents within the convent that went against Christian morality, it disturbed her greatly. She was concerned about the liaisons many inmates had built up with men outside the convent using their phones. She felt disquiet at the integrity and morality of monastic life being violated.

Her misgivings and concern led to her isolation too. One after another, incidents—most of them engineered—turned her into a persona non grata for the authorities. Her rewards were unexpected transfers to unpleasant locations. It took no time for the undesirable tendencies that had their origins in the convents to flow to the parishioners through the priests of the neighbourhood. Even when the source of the anonymous letters libelling some of the inmates was traced to the convent itself, the authorities chose to take no action.

Convinced that she could not lead such a conflicted life, she decided to quit the convent. Other nuns tried to dissuade her. The Provincial House also made similar overtures. She was also condemned to a solitary life in the convent's 'lock-up' for a month. Under the constant watch of the rest of the inmates, she had no freedom even to make phone calls. No one spoke to her either. She was compelled to eat ahead of others or after the others. Yet, she didn't yield.

Around that time, one of her teacher colleagues died of cancer. She was mother to two children, both infants. My sister decided to give the infants and the family a good life. It wasn't a decision taken on the spur of the moment; it was a decision taken serenely at the end of a year of prayer and contemplation. Kunjaanjaa wasn't in favour of her decision to quit the convent; in his opinion, it would besmirch the good name of the family. However, the ultimate decision lay with our mother; she stood firmly behind my sister in her decision.

What happened with my sister is a case in point: when adolescent girls or those just out of adolescence join monastic orders, often inveigled by the propaganda of evangelists, they are really surrendering all their liberties to the Church. Later, when the girls who have sacrificed their youth in the service of the Church want to return to lay life, it is not accepted by the Church. The individual's freedom is trampled upon with threats and attempts to influence family members. It is not merely mental duress; often, the girls even have to face physical abuse.

By branding them backsliders, the authorities will give ammunition to society at large to paint them as immoral women and humiliate them. My sister also had to go through this phase. Even natural justice is denied to a nun who ends her monastic life. She will be harried and made to look at her future with fear. Then she will be asked the portentous question of what her means of livelihood would be. After having lost all courage from spending the best part of her life in a convent without any freedom, an ordinary woman will not be able to find an answer for this easily. My sister, however, told them she would earn her livelihood as an agricultural labourer.

My father had paid twenty thousand rupees as patrimony when my sister became a nun. The authorities had received this sum from my father before she took on the habit. The quantum is usually based on the financial capability of parents. Since women had little inheritance rights in Christian families, an amount almost equal to what would have been paid as dowry was collected. Her patrimony was paid in 1980.

Once it was clear that there was no going back on her decision, the authorities tried to pass my sister on to her relatives without anyone knowing of it. They insisted on our brothers appearing before them. Our brothers were told to take her away late in the night or in the wee hours of the morning. Kunjaanjaa and my other brother, whom we used to call Kunjaangala, reached there early in the morning. In the meantime, some of the inmates had taken my sister, who was practically in solitary confinement, to another room through the back door. She was asked to return the habit she was wearing. What was given as a replacement was an ill-fitting churidar-kameez set, which was so dirty and smelly that she couldn't wear it. The drawstring of the churidar was missing. One of the nuns snipped off a piece from the cord that was part of her habit and gave it to my sister. The rosary and the crucifix were taken off her after this. All she got as reward for her quarter-century of evangelism was a reeking churidar-kameez set and two old nighties.

Once she was back in our home, there were enquiries from other well-to-do Christian families of Karikkottakary seeking her hand in marriage for their scions. However, my mother was against any alliance and insisted that she stick to her previous plan. My mother had already made enquiries about the widower whom my sister had set her heart upon, and she was ready only to give her blessings to a union where both partners had a good understanding. Thus, my sister's wish came true. She decided not to bear her own children and is now living happily as a mother of the two girls.

After she left monastic life, she had to suffer opprobrium from the Christian community and even our own family. Unable to suffer the humiliation of being branded a backslider, she left home and went to work as a maid in another place. She had to wait for three months before her wishes could be realized. The Church hampered her wedding plans too. It refused to give the letter relieving her of the vows, and my sister had to marry under civil law and have a registered marriage. Only after that could she start living with her new family. In her own words, this was the first time she was able to sleep peacefully and securely in the past twenty-five years.

Though she had given up her monastic life, she continued to live a prayerful life. She even detested the name Suma, given to her on her confirmation—so many were the bad memories she associated with it. I was not perturbed by her choices and stance in life. Since I was by then fully aware of life inside the convent, I felt no regret either.

*

The desire to live like Mother Teresa used to wash up in my mind in waves. I had once told the Provincial Superior that I wanted to donate my organs and apportion myself among the people. I had twice asked for permission to donate my kidneys. The first occasion was when the parents of a Class 3 student had come to the school seeking aid for his treatment. The second was when I came to know that a Class 9 student in Edathua needed kidneys from donors with a B+ve blood group. The congregation never granted permission.

Chapter Thirty

My sister and I had led our monastic lives in separate provinces. So none of the allegations or gossip against my sister used to reach me on time. However, in the outrage fomented against me, her dropping out of the convent was used as ammunition. In a way, the first step of monastic life is to uproot one's life and character and transplant them into an entirely different milieu, cutting away all previous ties. My experience teaches me that this is impossible.

> *For there is nothing covered that will not be revealed, or hidden that will not be known.*
>
> Luke 12:2

It is anti-human to renounce biological urges. Therefore, it is abhorrent to the Creator too. Though one may ardently desire to renounce material pleasures, I doubt if a complete distancing from them is achievable. I have seen this inclination in many of my fellow nuns. They revel in human emotions. The majority of nuns fail in staunching or even neutralizing the feelings of love, hatred and despair. This is the root cause of the discord that arises within the cloisters and within the monastic community.

Nuns take on new names to liberate themselves from their bygone memories. I broke with that tradition also. Though there was no concerted action, except for two nuns in our whole batch, none assumed new names. Only Omana and Achamma, perhaps not overly fond of their own names, chose to receive new names.

Experience has taught me one cannot escape worldly pleasures or succeed in forsaking them. When one lives in a society, there are many opportunities to face and fall prey to temptation. To be rid of them is next to impossible. We shall take cinema as an example. Irrespective of whatever restrictions are imposed on it, cinema as a source of entertainment cannot be separated from modern-day dilemmas. While working as a teacher, one may be compelled to watch movies while accompanying the students or as part of the pedagogy. Entertainment programmes or performance art forms telecast through TV, as another visual medium, cannot be ignored either. There have been occasions when one had to watch movies while on study trips or in the company of the vicar. Every art form is a manifestation of God's omnipresence.

The Franciscan order was built upon the belief of moving with the world. Obedience, chastity and poverty are considered to be enriching facets of life. However, today, the hallmark of Christian churches is such a centralization of money power that they have no moral right even to utter the word 'poverty'. This wealth is used to buttress political power.

I came to realize rather late what is meant by obedience. Obedience in the Church means acknowledgement of the imposition of the Holy See's will and the total negation of one's own wishes and aptitudes. As a person, what takes place is spiritual diminution and enfeeblement. A nun's character is annihilated through capitulation to the selfishness of the authorities and the consequent loss of her soul. Slavery and bondage are not obedience.

The conception is that monasticism is the heart of the Holy See. Pronouncements about the Christian spirit declaim policies and decisions that supposedly secure the interests of nuns. This is a myth. The only thing that happens without outside intervention is the performance of monastic duties in the convent. Every convent is a microcosm of this system. On paper, the See has no role in the governance of nuns' orders and convents. The clergy's role is limited purportedly to edification and benediction. This was conceived for free governance. However, nothing can move in a convent without the permission of the clergy. The nuns are compelled to surrender themselves and be subjugated.

One set of nuns turns silent in the face of unheeded opinions. Even when they want to speak out, most remain silent. The strong desire to stay on the right side of the authorities makes them forget and turn a blind eye to everything. If there is any breach of this unwritten protocol, loss of power is assured. Chances are that whatever little is in hand would also be forfeited. Notwithstanding that equality is the promised policy, nuns are mere instruments. They have no option but to accept servility. They accept their own weakness meekly and hand over the right to trample them to the others.

I know many nuns who have had to sacrifice their self-respect. Some of them, who have been publicly lauded and have won recognition, are facing severe repression in their non-public lives. The Church authorities, and even the convent authorities, are unwilling to cede to the individual the right to decide what she should study. One of our respected teachers, who happens to be a nun, confessed to me tearfully her tribulations. She was a professor, but the subject of her studies had been chosen by the hierarchy. She had told me that, at least on four occasions, decisions were taken out of her hands.

Convents outside Kerala are more considerate towards human feelings and take a more liberal approach to dissent. Neither the convent authorities nor the Church try to repress opinions or damn those who have a different opinion. There they believe that the only solution is to increase the frequency and length of prayers.

Chapter Thirty-One

On many occasions, I have been a mute witness to nuns taking refuge in prayer to overcome their sexual feelings and impulses, expressing their inborn sexual desires. The majority of the nuns who have left their home and families behind, and forsaken personal relationships so that they can lead a monastic life, are incapable of controlling their natural human urges. Many a time, I have been a spectator to their gesticulations and overtures.

Most of the nuns have relationships—proscribed by the Catholic Church—with priests. The status and power that priests hold in a convent's running and all through a nun's life are what facilitate this. Many of my companion nuns have had and continue to have such affairs. They will use their private moments to further them, spending hours together on the phone. There are ample instances of invisible patriarchy being exercised by male priests over the nuns. I know of regular sexual relations between priests and nuns.

One of the priests, a college teacher, used to often go to rest in a nearby convent. He had been given a room of his own. His declamations used to be on the protection to be taken before entering into sexual congress. The nuns were required not to be a mere audience. One of the sisters, fed up with the 'practical' classes she was compelled to participate in, confided in one of her male friends. However, he was helpless and couldn't intervene. Until he retired from his teaching job, this priest continued to give a thorough grounding on safe sex to all the nuns of that convent.

The daughter of one of my friends, a postgraduate student, had approached me for some help with her academics. I directed her to a priest who was proficient in her subject. I accompanied my friend and her daughter when they went to meet him. I left early, as I had to attend to some work in the church. They called me afterwards and thanked me for the help.

The next day the girl received a call from the priest asking after her welfare. Innocent as she was, she said she was keeping well. The priest began to give a passionate, amorous sermon. He said he wanted to kiss her body on three places below her neck. His lewdness completely threw her. She cried out, called her mother and handed over the phone to her. This incident upset the family very much and they complained to me. They called him directly and expressed their outrage in no uncertain terms. The family could be mollified only after several days of conciliation efforts by me. Finally, it subsided with him apologizing to them.

A nun who had been ravished by a priest in the vicarage confessed to me. She had joined the monastery along with me. In her case, the sexual exploitation had caused her no distress and she had actually enjoyed it. This remains one of the rarest of instances.

A young man had once remonstrated to me about a liaison between his aunt, who was a nun, and the parish priest. He told me that this very priest used to advise him constantly to be virtuous and celibate and not stray as he was a bachelor.

During the special confession sessions at the silent retreat, her voice filled with pain, a nun confessed to me about fondling a novice. During the Sacrament of Penance, too, some of the priests have a lecherous approach to the nuns who come to them to confess their sins to God.

I can say on the basis of what has been revealed to me from time to time that what appears in the press about the goings-on in convents is unfortunately true and correct. I know of convents where nubile nuns are sent to the priests. The kind of depravity these young nuns are subjected to in the vicarage is horrendous. This includes having to remain naked for hours together as the libidinous priests have their way with them. Some of the priests are such sex maniacs they do not stop even when the exhausted nuns plead with them that they cannot go on any more. These incidents have been narrated to me by some of the victims.

From many sources, I also know of senior nuns who use the young ones for sex. Often, the counselling that the victims choose to undergo to alleviate the mental trauma caused by such incidents becomes another cross they have to bear. The counsellors, who are mostly male priests, also constantly pursue these nuns for their own sexual gratification.

A young nun who accompanied a senior nun to the vicarage once had a bizarre experience. The priest lifted the girl onto his lap and fondled her for many hours. She confessed to me that this seduction made her also lustful, and it ended in carnal relations.

The experience of a brother too, who was abused by homosexual priests in the seminary and lost his mental balance, is tragic. For a whole year, he had to suffer through the depravity. Clinically depressed, he returned home and gave up monastic life. Another seminarian, too, has confessed to me that he had a similar experience. This young man, just out of his childhood, was set upon by the priest in charge of the seminary; the priest had wanted to sodomize him. When the boy resisted, the priest tied him to the bed and had his way. Fearful and unable to tell his family of this trauma, the boy asked for a transfer out of that seminary and moved to another one.

It would be wrong to think that only monastic orders under the Syro-Malabar Church have these ills. As can be seen from reports and other witness accounts, Christian monastic orders more often than not have pockets of licentiousness and degeneracy. Sexual exploitation and immorality are rampant. The mansions and cathedrals built with money collected within the country and abroad are monuments of hypocrisy. By collecting money from believers for consecrations and sacraments, the priests keep accumulating funds for the Church. The primary purpose of the priests' apostolic activities is to collect money—in the name of sacraments, funeral rites, novenas and saints' days, and for house-warming, consecration, and the like—whereas they should be serving the faithful without any pecuniary considerations.

The sermons given by these very priests turn off the audience. Their audience is suffering in silence, cursing the imposition on them, unable to respond. There are many instances of immature priests' fulminations—masquerading as gospel—breaching the limits of decency. A sermon given by the vicar at Karakkamala is an example of this: 'I have been consecrating homes in our parish … I am thankful for the affection, hospitality, cleanliness and respect you have given me. However, one of the homes I visited recently hadn't been swept for days. Scraps of food were lying around in every room. I had to consecrate the home while keeping my nose covered…'

I thought that those words came out of overflowing insensitivity and arrogance. It was evident from his humiliating words that this was no consecration to bless that family. Instead of instructing the family on the importance of cleanliness, what he had done was to denigrate it in front of the whole parish.

One of the priests, during a youth retreat, similarly gave a talk that was prurient. He was talking about his putative efforts to bring together a warring couple who had stopped talking to each other. After reaching their home, he said, he chose first to quiz the woman.

'Father,' she protested, 'must I share my body with that drunkard? He stinks so much; I won't do it.' The man had a different version. 'Father, tell her to wash her nightie once in a while ... I can't sleep with her because of the odour.' This 'revelation' was made in a group that consisted of children whose ages ranged between three and a half and seventeen years.

Priests use many stratagems to sneak into convents under the cover of darkness. The ostensible reason for the visit is to meet one of their acquaintances. They have a merry time in the convent's guest room. Food, and everything else, is served as if to royalty. Then starts the hours-long safe and secure sex with the chosen friend. Everything reaches a happy conclusion when early in the morning before departure he hands over a framed photo of the Holy Ghost to Mother Superior. 'Father ... What a beautiful, uplifting image ... Where did you get this from? We are lucky! We shall be mounting it here for keeps,' the ecstatic nuns will prattle on.

Many more have confessed to me first-hand accounts along these lines; others who have had people tell them these things have also told me of similar instances. The experience of a nun from another order is a prime example. She was working in an institution managed by one of the archdioceses. Her colleagues were priests. After a while, she reached the Provincial House claiming to suffer from severe stomach pain. At the hospital, after the initial assessment, she was taken straight to the labour room. After she delivered the child, the Church asked the family members to take her back. The priest, the father of that child, still continues with his priestly duties with impunity.

Chapter Thirty-Two

I TOO HAVE BEEN SEXUALLY MOLESTED FOUR TIMES BY PRIESTS. THE FIRST perpetrator was my former classmate from my Dharmaram Vidya Kshetram days in Bangalore, but it didn't happen during my time there. I shared a good, candid friendship with this brother, for whom I had a lot of respect and admiration. That turned out to be a curse. My nature was to keep my personal friendships within strict limits. This was not merely with men but even with the nuns in my order. As a child, I had followed this policy.

On average, even over the phone, I had not been in touch with this friend from Dharmaram more than once in a year. Then, once when he came to Mananthavady for apostolic work, he chose the Dwaraka convent, where I was an inmate, for his stay. It was night when he reached; as he appeared to be exhausted from the journey, I opened the guest room for him. I heated the water for his bath. When I reached the room, he had already entered the bathroom. Wanting to deliver the bucket of hot water up to the door of the bathroom, I entered the room.

He came out of the bathroom and tried to stop me from leaving the room. He touched my hand and kept kissing my forehead and cheeks fervently. Taken by surprise, I was rooted to the spot for a few seconds. He embraced me tightly. He fondled and caressed me. I lost my sense of time; I can't recall how long it went on. I heard my inner voice telling me to control the emotions that were surging within me. I regained my senses, pushed him away and protested. By that time, he also seemed to have found himself. He muttered the words, 'Okay ... Okay ...'

I was in great distress when I reached my room. However, I felt no guilt whatsoever. I was perplexed by the unexpected happening. Very soon, I regained my equanimity.

In such fraught situations, however, not every nun would be able to resist, more so if power dynamics are involved. This is what seems to have happened in the case in which Bishop Franco is the accused. His sexual predation was reported to be on a nun who had been assigned to iron his clothes and arrange them. In such an event, a nun may be left with no option but to capitulate.

The solution is to remove the unnatural restraints on human impulses and, with a liberal mindset, create licit avenues for the release of pent-up libido. The Church should pave the way for priests and nuns who, if interested, may marry and settle down as man and wife. They can live as partners in the chapel house. The Church must move with the times and reconcile itself to the enlightened view that the vestry may be the bedroom also; it is not an irreconcilable dichotomy.

This way, the ones who are asexual could then be allowed to carry on with God's work unmolested and in relative peace.

Chapter Thirty-Three

During one of my furloughs from Bhilwara, when I had come to the Mananthavady Provincial House, I decided to learn to play a musical instrument. I chose a priest proficient in playing the electronic keyboard to be my guru. He had friendly relations with all the nuns in my group except me. Coming to know of my wish, they had recommended him to me. One evening, I reached the retreat centre where he was the head. He welcomed me warmly and showed me to the room meant for me.

In the night, as I was bored by the inactivity, I decided to take a bath. My door was locked and I started to undress. There was a knock on the door; I opened the door only halfway, but he somehow squeezed in. As my irritation was apparent, he presented a lame excuse—that he had come to enquire about my dinner. He asked me if I would like to have ice cream and I replied in the affirmative. He left after this exchange.

At dinnertime, when I went to the dining hall, there he was again waiting for me. After dinner, he passed me some ice cream. I realized that he was touching my hand on purpose. He tried to nudge the conversation towards lasciviousness and ribaldry. Fully conscious of his intentions, I said nothing that could even remotely encourage him.

When the keyboard lessons started, he kept touching my body all the time; not just my torso, he pressed my thighs too. I dodged him, shook him off and conveyed my displeasure. I said I had no interest in him other than learning to play the keyboard.

Though I didn't fulfil my dream of being able to play a musical instrument, I returned to my convent. The first thing I did was delete his number from my phone. I never contacted him thereafter.

My third experience of harassment was at Gudalur in Tamil Nadu. One night I was forced to stay back at the church where I had gone to give religious instruction. I was given a room near the vicarage. I bade the vicar—who was from the Congregation of the Carmelites of Mary Immaculate—goodnight and entered my room. I was about to shut the door when he reappeared suddenly and entered the room. He started to make passes at me; not amused, I asked him to leave. When he tarried, I physically pushed him out of the room. I was filled with more courage, having passed yet another test successfully. I complimented myself on my ability to get out of such tricky circumstances unscathed.

Later, I did an assessment of all three incidents. In all these cases, the men had schemed well in advance and then sprung the trap. None of them were momentary lapses of discretion or self-control.

I had a similar experience at Dwaraka. The suggestive gestures of a priest at the dinner table made me uneasy. He was much younger than I was. Sitting across from me, he pressed his feet against my feet and started to caress them. I pulled my feet away and gave him a piece of my mind. I told him that nuns are not to be subjected to such treatment.

All that seemed to be so much water off a duck's back. He started again to touch me and feel my legs with his own. I repeated my advice; I raised my voice and said firmly that nuns are not for people like him to make passes at, at will. I have never again interacted with that lothario. I put an end even to telephonic contact.

Chapter Thirty-Four

Before Bishop Franco Mulakkal took centre stage, Robin Vadakkumchery was another clergyman that brought public disgrace to the Catholic Church and laity. He had sexually exploited and impregnated an underage girl from a poor family of his parish in Kottiyoor, about 26 kilometres away from Mananthavady, famous for the Shiva temple in the middle of a pond. He had many admirers among nuns too. The Church stood by the priest, despite the dishonour and infamy brought on the community by him and his actions. The Church authorities conspired to save him from prosecution.

No one in the convent showed any empathy for the unfortunate girl. They kept blaming and insulting her and her family. Robin was very close to a majority of the nuns in the convents, and it was amply clear that some of them were in a relationship with him, a relationship that went far beyond what was sanctioned by the Church. The leading player was a nun from my own convent. She used to be on the phone with Robin around the clock. However, she was not the only one. Even in the Provincial House, there were many nuns who were extremely close to Robin.

I used to see Robin occasionally at Vianney Bhavan, a hospice he used to visit on and off. I felt no inclination to strike up a friendship with him. Once, he spoke to me over the phone. The nub of the conversation was that whatever help I needed, he was ready to render. While I didn't reject the offer outright, I ended the conversation with a tepid response—that I would let him know if I needed any help.

A large group of nuns used to encircle him, charmed by his personality and smartness. His strategy was to pose as innocuous and straightforward. Separate plates are usually maintained in every convent for priests who have their food there. He would refuse such pandering. He would say that he would eat out of the same plates used by the nuns. The nuns would swarm around him. Since I always looked askance at his nature and intentions, I never joined the horde. Many tears were shed by nuns, both in the convent and in the Provincial House, mourning the fall of Robin. He was sentenced in 2019 to twenty years in prison, before the jail term was subsequently reduced to ten. Incidentally, other clergymen also looked up to him with admiration.

After Robin was jailed, the public relations officer (PRO) of the diocese, Father Thomas Joseph Therakam, was also prosecuted. Some senior nuns also had to face prosecution in cases connected to the safety of the child Robin had fathered. They received bail only after a protracted legal battle. Father Therakam curiously got away with a simple dismissal; he was dropped from the chairmanship of the District Child Welfare Committee. To me, as well as to those who have understood how the system works, it appeared that some sort of a Faustian deal had transpired behind the scenes. The involvement of Church and government authorities could not be ruled out. Though they seemed to have found enough legal loopholes to salvage most of their people, neither the Church nor the nuns were ready for any kind of soul searching or honest introspection.

When Father Noble Thomas took over from Father Therakam as the diocese's PRO, what we witnessed was him acting as an unabashed mouthpiece for the Church hierarchy. He spent plenty of time trying to counter my social media posts in an organized manner through the concerted efforts of his minions. He was the chief planner and architect of their attempts to discredit and destroy me through character assassination.

He was aided and abetted in this by the members of the Province of Mananthavady as eager accomplices. They disinterred and dusted off my records that lay buried in the convent archives. My companions and colleagues at the convent had no hesitation in passing over to Noble Thomas the complaints against me and my responses, much of which was only to be expected in over three decades of one's monastic life. They used the footage from the CCTV cameras that had been installed in the convent to slander me. They even circulated morphed videos through social media to defame me.

Chapter Thirty-Five

Not many days are left before I retire as a schoolteacher. I am now a persona non grata and an outcast as far as the Church is concerned, notwithstanding the fact that I have spent three-fourths of my life serving God and following Jesus Christ's path. I am what my experiences made me; I cannot forsake my character so formed. Neither do I have any illusion that the Church will show me any mercy.

A missive has already been received from the Vatican. They are proceeding step by step to throw me out. I am aware that there are no chances of a détente. A life compromised and subjugated is a life unliveable. I am sure that true believers and followers of Jesus Christ are behind me in this battle. My war doesn't end here.

I thank the Lord for my life of dedication, into which I had stepped with brave, unfaltering steps, as I continue marching ahead resolutely, upholding honesty and righteousness.

> *The high priest then asked Jesus about His disciples and His teaching.*

Jesus answered him, 'I spoke openly to the world. I always taught in the synagogue and in the temple, where the Jews always meet, and I said nothing in secret. Why do you ask Me? Ask those who heard Me and what I have said to them. Certainly they know what I said.'

When He had said this, one of the officers who stood by struck Jesus with the palm of his hand, saying, 'Is that how You answer the high priest?'

Jesus answered him, 'If I have spoken evil, bear witness of the evil, but if well, why do you strike me?' Then Annas sent Him bound to Caiaphas the high priest.

John 18:19–24

Appendix

Copy of the letter served on me by Father Sunil Thomas, Manager, Sacred Heart Higher Secondary School, Dwaraka suspending me.

Process by Manager, Sacred Heart Higher Secondary School
    Present: Father Sunil Thomas
    Sub: Aided School Teacher—Sister Lucy K.S. High School Assistant [HSA] (Mathematics), Disciplinary Action
    Suspension Order from Service Pending Enquiry

References:

1. Principal's report dated 28 September 2016
2. Manager's notice dated 13 October 2016
3. Undated reply from Sister Lucy
4. Principal's letter dated 27 October 2016

Order No 01/16 dated 1 November 2016

Following the report of the Principal [Ref 1] that Sister Lucy, HSA (Mathematics), Sacred Heart Higher Secondary School, has consistently failed in the performance of her official duties, and have repeatedly behaved irresponsibly and disrespectfully to the principal, she had been given a show cause notice.

For many days, Sister Lucy K.S. was not even ready to sign and acknowledge receipt of the same sent through the peon of the school. Further, till date she has also not abided by the repeated instructions of the principal and the manager to prepare and distribute the progress cards of 8H, which have been pending due to inaction on the part of the Sister Lucy. Ignoring the instruction that the reply to the manager's notice should be routed through the principal, Sister Lucy K.S. despatched it directly through registered post. Only after another written instruction was given to Sister Lucy has she given to the Principal a copy of her reply.

None of the explanations given by Sister Lucy K.S. in her response are satisfactory. She has acknowledged using the students of the class whose students can't even spell correctly to prepare the progress cards and has even justified the action. In the progress card, where the marks should have been based on 20, they were doubled (e.g. 36/20, 26/20 etc.) and recorded. Likewise, she has justified all her failings in the academic field. Most importantly, in this letter, she has cast aspersions on the principal, insulted her personally and made many unfounded allegations.

Prima facie, it is clear that as per provisions of the Kerala Education Rules, Chapter XIV A, it is imperative to hold further enquiries and institute disciplinary action against Sister Lucy K.S. for her culpable negligence in teaching and associated duties. It is also understood that for the smooth implementation of the disciplinary action, it is suspend her from the services.

Therefore, as provided in Section No 67 of the Kerala Education Rules, Chapter XIV A, Sister Lucy K.S., HSA Mathematics, Sacred Heart School is suspended with immediate effect from the services subject to further enquiries and disciplinary action. As provided in Section 67(8), the extension of the suspension beyond 15 days shall be subject to the preliminary investigation and findings by the District Education Officer.

During the period of suspension, Sister Lucy K.S. will be eligible for subsistence allowance as per the rules.

[Signed]
Father Sunil Thomas
[official stamp]
To
Sister Lucy K.S., HSA (Mathematics)
Sacred Heart Higher Secondary School
Dwaraka
Through the Principal

cc:

1. The principal (3 copies)
2. Sister Lucy K.S. maybe served the order and a copy with her dated acknowledgement should be returned.
3. A copy is submitted to District Education Officer along with the exhibits for further necessary action.

DEO's Order to withdraw the suspension

Procedure by Wayanad District Education Officer [T. Sankara Narayana Prasad]

Sub: Aided Public Education—Disciplinary Action against Sister Lucy K.S. HSA (Mathematics), Sacred Heart, HSS, Dwaraka—Order Ending the Suspension

Reference: School Manager's Order No. 01/2016 dated 1 Nov 2016

Order No. B4/9107/2016 dated 9 Nov 2016

As per the order referred to above, Sister Lucy K.S. has been suspended w.e.f. 1 Nov 2016 by the manager pending enquiry and permission has been sought to extend the suspension beyond fifteen days after conducting a preliminary investigation.

The suspension order has been passed in order to take disciplinary action for the alleged negligence/dereliction in official duties, irresponsible and rude behaviour with the principal, shortcomings in progress card preparation and late attendance in staff meetings.

A preliminary investigation was conducted on 4 Nov 2016 on these matters at the school. The manager, principal and the teacher against whom these charges have been made were present. The points made by all the parties were heard. After examining them, the following conclusion has been reached.

As per KER Chapter XIV A, Section 67, an aided-school employee can be suspended when disciplinary/punitive actions have been decided upon, punitive disciplinary actions are in process, or the employee is involved in some criminal case and its enquiry or trial is going on.

As per para 16(2) A of the Disciplinary Proceedings Manual, the seriousness of the charges, the need to suspend the employee for conducting the enquiry and the severity of punishment if the charges are proven as correct, should be taken into consideration to decide if the suspension is warranted and if the suspension should be extended. Further, the chances of evidence related to the charges being destroyed and loss of morality of the institution also should be taken into consideration.

The charges against the teacher in this case are not serious. For the purpose of gathering evidence on these charges, other witnesses are not needed. The teacher is not in a position to destroy any evidence that supports the charges. Even if the charges are proven, they are not sufficient to attract severe punitive action. There is no need to keep the teacher under suspicion in order to take disciplinary action on the charges.

Therefore, it is ordered hereby the suspension order on Sister Lucy K.S. may be cancelled with immediate effect. She should be taken back also into service with immediate effect. Disciplinary action may be taken by the Manager as per KER Section 67(8), Chapter XIV A.

[signed]
Personal Assistant of the District Education Officer
Full additional-charge, Wayanad District

cc:

1. Manager, Sacred Heart HSS, Dwaraka
2. Principal, Sacred Heart HSS, Dwaraka
3. Sister Lucy K.S. Mathematics Teacher, Sacred Heart HSS, Dwaraka
4. Record file

Order cancelling the Suspension Order

Procedure by Manager, Sacred Heart Higher Secondary School
Present: Father Sunil Thomas
Sub: Aided School Teacher—Sister Lucy K.S. High School Assistant [HSA] (Mathematics)
Suspension Order

References:

1. The Manager's Order No. 01/2016 dated 01 Nov 2016
2. The Wayanad District Education Officer's order B4/9107/2016 dated 09 Nov 2016

Order No. 01/2016 dated 14 Nov 2016

Disciplinary action had been initiated against Sister Lucy K.S., HSA (Mathematics) following serious charges levelled against her, and as per Ref 1 above, she had been placed under suspension pending enquiry.

As per Ref 2, the District Education Officer, who had conducted a preliminary hearing as per the regulations, found that there were no grounds to keep Sister Lucy K.S. under suspension, invalidated the suspension order, ordered that she should be taken back into service immediately and instructed that the disciplinary actions could continue.

In these circumstances, subject to [the] final decision on the disciplinary action against her, Sister Lucy K.S. HSA (Mathematics) is being given permission to re-join duty, by cancelling her suspension as per Section 67 (8) of the Chapter XIV A of the KER. The principal may take further necessary action in this regard and should report the day Sister Lucy K.S. joins back her duty.

As per the permission given by the DEO, the disciplinary action against her will be completed in due course and as per the regulations.

Father Sunil Thomas
[official stamp]

To,
Sister Lucy K.S. HSA (Mathematics) [under suspension]
Through the Principal

cc: The Principal. A copy of this may be got acknowledged by Sister Lucy K.S. with date and returned.

The District Education Officer, Wayanad, for his information.

[Kerala Government letterhead]
Summary

Public Education—Aided Schools—Order on the Revision Petition of the School Manager seeking extension of the suspension of Sister Lucy K.S. HSA [Mathematics] Teacher at the Sacred Heart Higher Secondary School, Wayanad District.
Public Education Department (A)
G.O. (RT.) No. 913/2017/Po.V.
Thiruvananthapuram
31 March 2017

Ref: 1. Revision Petition dated 17 Nov 2016 from the Manager, Sacred Heart School, Mananthavady
2. Letter no. EM(5)/4566/17/DPA dated 31 Jan 2017 issued by Public Education Director
3. Letter no. B2/848/17 dated 1 February 2017 issued by Deputy Director Education, Wayanad
4. Letter no. B4/9107/2016 dated 28 Jan 2017 issued by Wayanad District Education Officer

Order

Father Sunil Thomas had submitted a revision petition to the Hon'ble Minister of Education requesting re-examination of the Wayanad District Education Officer's cancelling the suspension order of Sister Lucy K.S., HSA mathematics teacher, Sacred Heart School, Dwaraka, Mananthavady Division, pending investigation of the serious lapses in performance of her academic duties. Following the Hon'ble Minister's orders to listen to the petitioners in person before arriving at a decision, the Under Secretary met the petitioners in person on 2 February 2017.

At the time of the hearing, the concerned parties had submitted the following contentions: The manager had alleged that Sister Lucy K.S.,

HSA teacher [of mathematics], refused to acknowledge the headmistress of the school, had progress cards prepared by the students, continuously failed in her official duties, made parents sign on the attendance register etc. In addition, he also alleged that on being informed by the headmistress that Sister Lucy continued to behave defiantly and disrespectfully with her, when she was served a notice, she refused to receive and acknowledge the same and the response was sent directly by registered post, instead of routing it through the headmistress as directed. Additional allegations made were that once Sister Lucy had abandoned the leftover question papers and additional answer sheets in the examination hall, wrong messages were spread by her through her mobile phone and she had been careless while preparing marksheets.

Sister Lucy had submitted the following explanations against the charges laid by the Manager: The allegations against Sister Lucy, who had been teaching in Sacred Heart School from 1997, were made for the first time only after the current incumbent had taken charge as headmistress; on 27 September 2016, when the PTA (Parent–Teacher Association) meeting for Class 10H had taken place, all thirty-nine students and their parents had come and met Sister Lucy, and this was recorded by her in the subject evaluation sheet—these were stated by Sister Lucy. Since she had not received the notification, on the afternoon of 20 September 2016, she could not participate in the staff meeting. However, the next day she had seen and signed the minutes of the meeting. It was also submitted that only because the marks of various subjects were received late, the progress reports had to prepared on an emergency basis with the help of two students, and because of an inadvertent oversight only two question papers and two plain sheets from a unit test conducted for Class Ten were left behind in the examination hall. Further, after twenty years of sincere, dedicated service when she received a memo, she had been unable to read it in the school so it was read only at the convent, and the next two days being Saturday and Sunday, her reply was given on Monday. Since the mark record book was found missing from the staff room, she expressed her suspicion that it had been removed by someone on purpose. Sister Lucy has admitted that the attendance of the latecomers for the 8H PTA meeting had been recorded using a pencil in the attendance register. She has also stated that she had only forwarded the message received on her phone.

However, the Wayanad District Education Officer had ruled that for disciplinary action to be taken against the teacher for these transgressions, she need not remain under suspension, which should be withdrawn. The same has been approved by the Public Education Officer and the Deputy Director of Education, Wayanad. However, dissatisfied with the same, the Manager had submitted an application to the District Education Officer to hold a detailed enquiry as per KER Chapter 14, A Rule 75 on the charges against Sister Lucy. The Manager has demanded that, till this enquiry is completed, the teacher should remain under suspension.

Sister Lucy has been a teacher for almost twenty years in the Sacred Heart Higher Secondary School. It is understood that only after Mrs Molly Joseph had taken charge as headmistress during the 2015–16 academic year that allegations were made against this teacher, by misguiding the management. Sister Lucy informed that she had conveyed her dissatisfaction to the management at someone who had no qualifications and were held in low esteem by other staff members for being appointed as the headmistress superseding other senior teachers. It may be personal animosity generated by this complaint that [...] led to the headmistress making allegations against Sister Lucy. Hoping to get good results for class 10H, every day, from 9 a.m. to 10 a.m. extra classes are being taken[, which] shows the sincerity of the teacher. These allegations which apparently are born out of only personal enmity against Sister Lucy, who has been handling mathematics and IT subjects for Class Ten and who has been a teacher in the same school for twenty years[...] Moreover, such problems may affect students' academics to a great extent.

An application has been submitted to the Wayanad District Education Officer as per KER Chapter 14, A Rule 75 to hold a detailed enquiry into the allegations against the teacher, following his directive as per KER Section 67(8) Chapter 14 to take the teacher back in service and continue disciplinary action. It can be understood from this that for the detailed enquiry to be conducted against Sister Lucy, she need not continue to be under suspension.

Based on the circumstances described above, the order is being issued approving the directive of the Wayanad District Education Officer that for a detailed enquiry to be conducted against Sister Lucy, the mathematics HSA teacher in Sacred Hearts Higher Secondary School, she need not continue to be under suspension, and rejecting the revision petition filed by the school manager that she should continue to be under suspension till completion of the enquiry. At the same time, since teachers are obliged to acknowledge and obey the headmistress as a superior authority in the school, the proceedings on the revision petition are being ordered close with a warning is being issued to Sister Lucy that in future such failings should not recur on her side.

[as per the order of the Governor]
B. Shreekala
Under Secretary

1. Sister Lucy K.S., HSA (Mathematics), Sacred Heart Higher Secondary School, Dwaraka, Nalloornad P.O., Mananthavady, Wayanad 670645
2. Manager, Sacred Heart Higher Secondary School, Dwaraka, Nalloornad P.O., Mananthavady, Wayanad 670645
3. Public Education Director, Thiruvananthapuram
4. Deputy Director Education, Wayanad
5. District Education Officer, Wayanad
6. Principal Accountant General (Audit, A&E) Kerala, Thiruvananthapuram
7. Record file/Office copy

As per orders
-sd
Section Officer

Application Submitted for Permission to Buy a Car

From:
Lucy Kalapura
Karakkamala

To,
The Provincial Team,
Deepthi Bhavan,
Mananthavady
Respected Sister. Provincial and Team
Sub; My Apostolic Work

I need to enhance the responsibilities I have as a teacher. I need to specially visit the homes of the students and study their circumstances. I require a vehicle to do this conveniently. This would also be useful for visiting parishioners' homes and during emergencies in the convent. We would also not need to waste time waiting for the bus [if a car is purchased]. Therefore, I request that you grant me dispensation to own such a vehicle.

28 May 2018

Letter Rejecting Application to Own a Car

[FCC letterhead]

Prot. No. 32/2018
4 June 2018

Dear Respected Sister Lucy Kalapura,
Grace and peace to you in the name of God our Creator.
    The application dated 28 May 2018 addressed to Apostolic Team and submitted by you on a plain sheet of paper for the purchase of a car to

be used to make the performance of your apostolic work easier has been discussed in the Provincial Council on 2 June 2018.

Sister Lucy has written that those in the teaching profession should be made more responsible and that *greater sincerity should be shown for the salary that is paid by the government.*[*] Certainly, these two are necessary. The letter also says that to visit the students' homes and understand their environs and for convenient travel, a vehicle is necessary. In normal circumstances, such travels are undertaken by using a bus or autorickshaw. As a senior member of the Church, Sister Lucy has already expressed on innumerable occasions her fears that our monasticism is turning into life of luxurious extravagance and the Church is losing its soul. As senior members of the order, each one of us must ensure that the supreme soul of the Church is not lost and others see us as paragons of simple life. That should be the way we show our commitment to the Church and the order of which we are members. Further, it is hoped that Sister Lucy is aware that the Mananthavady Province synaxis's decision is that a vehicle need not be bought even for common use in the Province. It is hereby advised that due to these reasons, it is not possible to give such a sanction.

Yours faithfully,
Sister Stephina
[official stamp of Provincial Superior]
DEEPTHI BHAVAN

Warning Letters Issued by Mananthavady Provincial Superior

[FCC letterhead]

Prot. No. 16/2018
13 March 2018

---

[*] In the letter written by Sister Lucy in Malayalam, this is missing. Apparently, this has been added from the side of the Provincial Superior.

Dear Sister Lucy Kalapura,

Grace and peace to you in the name of God our Creator.

It has been noticed that for the last few years, Sister Lucy has adopted a lifestyle which does not conform to the Franciscan Clarist Congregation's monastic ways. Only after getting fully familiar with the regulations of the FCC and its routines have the vows been given and you have become a member of the order. As one who has been leading a monastic life for the past thirty-two years, it is presumed that you are fully aware what is prescribed in the *Rule and Constitution of the Franciscan Clarist Congregation* and the *Way of Life of Franciscan Clarist Congregation* with respect to seeking permissions and handling money.

As per the rules and traditions of our order, when a transfer order is given to a sister via a Statement of Obedience, she has to move to the new station within eight days. The non-acceptance of the Statement of Obedience, which was served on Sister Lucy in April 2015, is an instance of significant violation of the vow of obedience. In October 2016 when Sister Lucy received an order on disobedience from the authorities at the Dwaraka school where she is a teacher; she hadn't informed the Provincial Superior about the same. Moreover, without informing the authorities of this order, she even filed a complaint against the principal to higher-ups in the Education Department.

When informed by the school authorities, I spoke to Sister Lucy, counselled her and advised her, making a list of things she had to abide by. That she never replied to my letter of 21 December 2016, wherein I had specifically asked for a response, is proof that she didn't heed the advice. I am certain that Sister Lucy, experienced as she is in monastic ways, is well aware that a nun's way of asking for a permission from her superiors is not akin to writing a social media (e.g. WhatsApp) message. Yet, Sister Lucy's practice of using WhatsApp messages as notifications and then considering them as approvals during the past two years is a gross violation of the vow of obedience.

On 4 May 2017, I had received a WhatsApp message from Sister Lucy that she had done some 'paper work' and that Sophia Books would be publishing it. The message contained a few poems written by her. After seven months, on 21 Dec 2017, another WhatsApp message arrived, 'It's been more than one-and-a-half years since I have been asking for permission and blessings to publish my book. In between I also expressed an opinion that I should release a CD. Therefore hoping to receive the permission and that a few months' salary should be considered as social work.' Sister Lucy's decision to spend money as per her will is a gross violation of *The Rule and Constitution of the Franciscan Clarist Congregation of the Syro-Malabar Major Archiepiscopal Church* No. 26 and the *Way of Life of Franciscan Clarist Congregation* no. 27.

Our constitution clearly states that after a nun has taken her vows, whatever she earns or comes by will be considered as wealth of the Church. Likewise, in the *Way of Life of Franciscan Clarist Congregation*, the remuneration she receives for her occupation or as a personal gift or donation all should be handed over to the superior and added to the common funds. When in the order no one other than those authorized to handle money can do so as per its rules; it is against the principles of monasticism to use one's salary as per one's wishes after merely shooting off a WhatsApp message.

It was also improper for her to use my name at the launch of the CD titled *Devalayam*. On 25 October 2017, Sister Lucy had written me a personal letter asking for permission and funds to publish her poems as a book. After I had read the poems, I had told her that we shall think about publishing it as a book after sending it to the Church's publications.

Later, on 3 October 2018, when I had summoned Sister Lucy to Deepthi Bhavan to meet her I had asked if I may be given a hard copy of her collection of poems, and I had been promised the same; till date I have not received it. I had informed Sister Lucy as per our *Way of Life of Franciscan Clarist Congregation* (No 168) the permission of the local hierarch was required before publishing a book. Disobeying all this, Sister Lucy took actions of her own accord to publish the book, and on 10 March 2018 through a WhatsApp message I was informed that *Snehamazhayil,* a book of poems, was ready and the fifty thousand rupees spent on it should be considered apostolic expenses. This is a violation of the vows of obedience and poverty.

Dear Sister Lucy, I am informing you that you should not repeat these unmonastic activities of yours and you should be ready to live by the *Rule and Constitution of the Franciscan Clarist Congregation* and the *Way of Life of Franciscan Clarist Congregation*. I would like to also inform you that if you continue to repeat such actions, we shall have to consider your dismissal from the order and similar punitive actions. Within one week of receipt of this letter, I should receive your reply by Registered Post (and not through WhatsApp).

Yours faithfully,
Sister Stephina
[official stamp of Provincial Superior]

[FCC letterhead]

Prot. No. 18/2018
28 March 2018

Dear Sister Lucy Kalapura,
    Grace and peace to you in the name of God our Creator.

On 11 March 2018, a registered letter (Prot. No. 16/2018) had been sent to Sister Lucy with instructions that within one week of receipt of the letter a reply should be sent by registered post. This reminder is being sent because to date (28 March 2018) no reply has been sighted.

Dear Sister Lucy, as mentioned in the previous letter, you are again informed that you should not repeat the unmonastic activities that you have indulged in, and you should be ready to live according to the *Rule and Constitution of the Franciscan Clarist Congregation* and the *Way of Life of Franciscan Clarist Congregation*.

You are also hereby informed that if you continue to act in the same vein, you shall be subjected to punitive action, including dismissal from the order. It is again requested that within one week of receipt of this letter a written reply be sent through registered post, and not through WhatsApp.

Sister Stephina
[official stamp of Provincial Superior]
cc: The Superior General & Council

Reply from Sr Lucy to the Provincial Superior's Letters

Dear Sisters,

I am a person who lives and abides by the charism of FCC and one who does good for the others, especially the poor. The contents of the following registered letters—Prot. No. 16/2018 dated 13 March 2018; Prot. No. 18/2018 dated 28 March 2018—received by me are not in keeping with the truth. Further, the repeated threats that steps will be taken to expel me from the order is causing me mental trauma.

I am proud that I am undergoing this because I did apostolic work and social service. If God permits, I want do as much good work as I can. Therefore my decision is that I must use all the talents (intellectual, mental, spiritual and artistic) gifted to me by God in the service of God's people. Is this against the charism and ways of the order? I must live a life as per my beliefs, ideals and convictions.

Therefore, as indicated in the letters received by me, if the apostolic work and the good deeds done have been found unacceptable by you, you are at liberty to take any decision that you want.

However, I should be provided for so I may lead an untroubled life. I should be compensated adequately for my thirty-two years of service. I should also receive full remuneration for the twenty-five years' hard work at the school.

Affectionately,
-sd
Lucy Kalapura
Karakkamala
4 April 2018

[FCC letterhead]

Prot. No. 31/2018
19 May 2018

Dear Sister Lucy Kalapura,

Grace and peace to you in the name of God our Creator.

The Franciscan Clarist Congregation is an order which has been granted pontifical status in the Eastern Catholic Major Archiepiscopal Church. It is regulated by the Code of Canons of the Eastern Churches (CCEO), Third Order Regular (TOR Rule) and its own constitution. The aim of the congregation is be witnesses of the poor and humble Jesus Christ before the whole world by publicly practising the vows of obedience, consecrated celibate chastity and poverty. The Mananthavady St. Mary's Province, established in 1988, is one of the provinces of the aforementioned Franciscan Clarist Congregation.

Sister Lucy Kalapura is someone who has studied and assimilated the Congregation's *Rule and Constitution of the Franciscan Clarist Congregation* and the *Way of Life of Franciscan Clarist Congregation* of the Syro-Malabar Major Archiepiscopal Church during her aspirancy; on 22 May 1985, of her own full volition, she took the temporary vows, accepted the habit and took up postulancy. On 21 May 1991, she took her perpetual solemn vows and joined the order permanently.

After I had become the Provincial Superior of Mananthavady Province, I came to know of Sister Lucy's impudent and rebellious actions, and discussed with her and counselled her orally as well as in writing to get her to amend her ways; I have even served a warning letter for this purpose. However, they have neither elicited a response nor did they seem to bring about any behavioural changes in her.

As a consequence, in its meeting on 4 March 2018, the Provincial Council studied and evaluated Sister Lucy's recalcitrant behaviour and sent her a registered letter on 13 March 2018, advising her also to reply only by postal mail. Since there was no response whatsoever to the abovesaid letter, the Provincial Council in its meeting on 25 March 2018 discussed the matter and decided that since there was no response, a reminder may be sent. Accordingly, a reminder letter was sent on 28 March 2018 by registered post.

When there was no response to both these letters, Sister Jyothi Maria, one of the Provincial Councillors, and I went to the Karakkamala convent on 5 April 2018 to meet Sister Lucy in person and talk to her. We met and after our discussions, on my return, I received a letter from Sister Lucy Kalapura through registered post, purportedly dated 4 April 2018.

What Sister Lucy has stated in this letter is untrue and are allegations drummed up to justify herself. A response is being given now to Sister Lucy's reply, after the Mananthavady Provincial Council evaluated the matters stated in Sister Lucy's letter, and because it recognizes that Sister Lucy should be aware of her actions against the order and the Church. There is adequate evidence to prove beyond any doubt that Sister Lucy's actions listed 1–6 below, which she in her letter has described as 'not keeping in with truth'.

1. After I became the Provincial Superior of the St. Mary's Province of Mananthavady, in April 2014, as per the decision of the Provincial Council, Sister Lucy was served a Statement of Obedience transferring her from the Kommayad convent to the Dwaraka convent. However, Sister Lucy refused to acknowledge and accept the transfer and showed public defiance. This has caused considerable strife to both the Church and the Catholic community at large. It is again reminded that such behaviour is a grave violation of the vow of obedience contained in the Franciscan Clarist Congregation's constitution.
2. Rule 124 of *The Rule and Constitution of the Franciscan Clarist Congregation of the Syro-Malabar Major Archiepiscopal Church*

says, 'The apostolic work should be appropriate and opportune to the will of the Church and our charism and subservient to monasticism and its authorities'. However, when there was a disciplinary issue at your apostolic space of Sacred Hearts Higher Secondary School, you did not respond to my letter personally delivered to you on 21 Dec 2016, and without the permission of the Provincial Council or myself, you filed a complaint with the education authorities against the management and the principal of the school. You are reminded that this act is defiance to authority.

3. Rule 101 of *The Rule and Constitution of the Franciscan Clarist Congregation of the Syro-Malabar Major Archiepiscopal Church* inter alia states, 'The habit is a symbol of dedication' and stipulates that members of the congregation wear clothes as described in Rule No 196. The members of the order who publicly accept the habit at the time of temporary vows, continue to wear the Franciscan Clarist Congregation's apposite monastic attire. When I came to know that when you had gone to Makkiyad for prayers and had attended the Holy Mass keeping aside the habit and wearing a churidar-kameez set, I had asked you for an explanation; your reply was, 'At least, I was wearing something.' This reveals your defiance and derision towards monastic life and your habit.

4. Rule 166 of *The Rule and Constitution of the Franciscan Clarist Congregation of the Syro-Malabar Major Archiepiscopal Church* states, 'The approval of the local hierarch is needed for publishing books.' However to publish *Snehamazhayil*, a book of your poems, you had not obtained the approval of the reverend father of Mananthavady Diocese. No approval was also obtained from neither the Provincial Superior nor the Provincial Council. The release of the book and the CD titled *Devalayam* are serious violations of your vows, committed in defiance of the Church and the congregation's rules.

5. Using my name without my knowledge or permission for the audio launch of the CD is a criminal offence and liable for prosecution.
6. As per Rule 26 of *The Rule and Constitution of the Franciscan Clarist Congregation of the Syro-Malabar Major Archiepiscopal Church*, 'Through their vows of poverty, sisters relinquish independent the handling and transaction of valuable articles. After the perpetual vows, all that is earned by the nun and she receives will belong to the Church.' As per Rule 23, 'Without the permission of the Superior, no gifts shall be accepted, donations given, property transacted, loans given or taken, anything taken or given in trust.' Rule 27 states, 'Everyone including Superiors shall be scrupulous in monetary transactions. No one who is not required by her occupation to do so, shall not handle money. All monies received as remuneration for her work or as personal gift shall be made over to the Superior and added to the common funds. In my letter of 13 March 2018, I have noted that from December 2017 till date, your salary been usurped by you and has been spent on your personal needs and for the fulfilment of your desires without the permission of the Provincial Council or myself; thus you acted and lived in unmonastic manner. Such acts on your side and your behaviour have caused the Congregation and the Church disrepute. I remind you of my previous words that these actions are unmonastic, and gravely violate the sanctity of a life bound by vows—especially that of poverty and obedience.

In your reply, your statement '…the repeated threats that steps will be taken to expel me from the order is causing me mental trauma' is extremely puerile. Rules 119 and 120 dictate corrective action and written warnings against grave misdemeanours, such as grievous transgressions in monetary transactions and disrespectful behaviour towards superiors. I would like to point out that this is not mental torture because when it is apparent that a member of the order is living by flouting the rules of the order, the Code of Canons of the Eastern Churches enjoins the Church authorities to remind her of the same, and if she does not abide by them, she should be served notices informing her that punitive actions will be taken if amends are not made.

I read your statement in your letter where you say: 'I am proud that I am undergoing this because I did apostolic work and social service.' After deviating from the laws of the order that you are a member of, if you release a CD on a whim and without the permission or blessings of the superiors, that does not count as apostolic work or social service. Not only that, this is its very antithesis. This is not in keeping with the charism of Franciscan congregation; it is also a grave infraction of the vows of poverty and obedience.

In your letter you have asked, 'Therefore my decision is that I must use all the talents (intellectual, mental, spiritual, artistic) gifted to me by God in the service of God's people. Is this against the charism and ways of the order?' Using God-given talents to serve God's people is never against the rules or charism of the order. All that is needed is that they should be carried out in consonance with the Church's rules and in deference to the Church authorities.

You have stated in your letter that 'I must live a life as per my beliefs, ideals, and convictions.' TOR Rule No. 25 says, 'Following the example of Our Lord Jesus Christ Who made His own will one with the Father's; the sisters and brothers are to remember that, for God, they should give up their own wills.' As said in Rule 14 'The evangelical counsel of obedience, undertaken in the spirit of faith and love in the following of Christ, who was obedient even unto death, obliges submission of one's will to lawful Superiors, who act in the place of God when they give commands that are in accordance with each institute's own constitution.' One's own beliefs, ideals and convictions need not be always good, monastic, or value-based. You must realize the truth that choosing to live by one's own beliefs, ideals and convictions is not the monastic way.

First Canonical Warning Letter Issued by Superior General

[FCC letterhead]
Superior General, Portiuncula, FCC Generalate
Prot. No. 01/2019
1 Jan 2019

To,
Sister Lucy Kalapura FCC,
FC Convent Vimala House,
Karakkamala, P.O. Wayanad,
Mananthavady

Sub: First Warning Letter to Sister Lucy Kalapura by Superior General

Dear Sister Lucy Kalapura,

Sister Lucy, you are a perpetually professed sister in the Franciscan Clarist Congregation belonging to the St. Mary's Province Mananthavady. I have received many allegations against you and witnessed some of them. For the past few years, you are leading a life that is against the principles of religious life and against the *Rule and Constitution of the Franciscan Clarist Congregation.* You have received several corrections and warnings from your Provincial Superior due to your unsuitable ways. (Ref. Prot. No. 16/2018, 18/2018, 31/2018)

1. On 10 May 2015, you have received a transfer order by the Statement of Obedience from your then Provincial Superior Stephina, which you have not obeyed. I remind you that any failure to comply with the transfer and appointment order amounts to wilful disobedience.
2. Your Provincial Superior had denied permission to publish your poems as a book. Yet you published your book *Snehamazhayil* without seeking the permission of the local hierarch.

3. The applications you had put for learning driving, getting a licence and buying vehicle were not sanctioned and permissions were not granted. But you learned driving, got a licence and bought a car, Maruthi [sic] Alto K10 VXT AMT (O) BS IV and registered it as KL-12-1/9719 in your name. Sister Lucy K.S., having taken a loan by approaching the headmistress without the permission and knowledge of your superiors. These are grave violations of the vow of obedience.
4. For the publication of the book, you have used fifty thousand rupees without proper permission; this exceeds the amount which even the Superior General of FCC can use for extraordinary expenses. Regarding the buying of the car, you have done what your Superior had asked you not to do in all seriousness and have administered a thing of very high monetary value (around four lakh rupees), which even the superior can administer only with the consent of the Council (*Rule and Constitution of the Franciscan Clarist Congregation* 26, 161, 162). You have also not entrusted your salary from December 2017 (See *Rule and Constitution of the Franciscan Clarist Congregation* no. 27). These are grave infringements of the vow of poverty.
5. Your deeds on 20 September 2018, and on the following days, were of most grave external scandal and harm to the Church and FCC. You went to Ernakulam High Court junction and participated in the protest held by the SOS Action Council without the permission of your Superior.
6. You have further published articles in some non-Christian newspapers and weeklies like *Mangalam* (on 22/23-10-2018), *Madhyamam* etc., gave [sic] interviews in *Samayam* without seeking permission from the Provincial Superior (see the *Rule and Constitution of the Franciscan Clarist Congregation* N. 166). Through facebook [sic], channel discussions, and in the articles, you have belittled the Catholic leadership by making false accusations against it and tried to bring down the sacraments. You tried to defame FCC

also. Your performance through social media as a religious sister was culpable of arising grave scandal. [sic]

You have received several warnings and corrections from your Provincial Superior for your improper behaviours and violations of religious discipline. Instead of correcting yourself, you are simply denying the allegations against you stating that you have to live by your own beliefs, ideologies,** and convictions. You are repeatedly violating the vows of obedience and poverty. You cannot live by your own beliefs, ideologies [sic] and convictions in FCC without respecting and keeping the values and traditions of FCC alive. The evangelization and social work you do should be according to the FCC values, principles and rules. The present mode of your life is a grave violation of the profession you have made.

I, as your Superior General, telephoned you in person on 28 November 2018 and expressed my desire to talk with you. Considering your inconvenience, I had asked you to give me a date so I could mark it in my diary. But you did not respond. Again I asked you fix a date to meet me in writing through my letter dated 12 December 2018. In your reply dated 16 December 2018, you did not give the date within the time limit mentioned, which was eight days. Instead you insist [sic] on fulfilling your own demands. This is clear defiance of authority and obstinate disobedience.

Hence, I, Sister Ann Joseph, Superior General of the Franciscan Clarist Congregation of which you are a member, hereby issue you the first canonical warning with the threat of dismissal from the Franciscan Clarist Congregation.

However, as a good shepherd, I am coming in search of you, and I humbly request you to stop your obstinate disobedience. I ask you to come to the Generalate of the Franciscan Clarist Congregation, Portiuncula Asokapuram on **9 January 2019 at 11 a.m. to meet me**

** In the letter written by Sister Lucy in Malayalam, she has used the word *aadarshangal*, which means 'principles' or 'ideals' and not 'ideologies'.

personally and rectify the grave faults you have made till now, observing the instructions placed before you by the Superior General of FCC. If you fail to reach the Generalate as required, it will be considered wilful refusal on your part to comply with a legitimate order of your major superior and the **next canonical steps as per norms of law will be taken.**

Once again inviting you to realize your mistakes and lead an exemplary life in FCC and wishing God's abundant blessings upon you.

Yours in our Lord,
-sd
Sister Ann Joseph FCC
[Stamp]

[FCC letterhead]
Superior General, Portiuncula, FCC Generalate

Prot. No. 12/2019
18 January 2019
'Surely Goodness and Mercy shall follow me all the days of my life.' (Ps 23:6)

To,
Sister Lucy Kalapura FCC
FC Convent Vimala Home,
Karackamala P.O. Wayanad
Mananthavady

Dear Sister Lucy Kalapura,

You being a perpetually professed member of the Franciscan Clarist Congregation belonging to the St. Mary's Province, Mananthavady were asked to come to the Generalate and meet me in person on 9 January

2019; the date was then prolonged [sic] up to 14 January 2019 for your convenience. But you have neither turned up nor given explanations to me; instead you appeared in the media to justify your scandalous act [of] violation against the *Rule and Constitution of the Franciscan Clarist Congregation* & the *Way of Life of Franciscan Clarist Congregation.* Several allegations persist against you as you are made known [sic] by the first canonical warning letter (Prot. No. 1/2019).

1. You have not obeyed my order as the Superior General to come and meet me in person.
2. You did not obey the transfer order dated 10 May 2015 by the Statement of Obedience from your Provincial. This is a grave violation of the vow of obedience.
3. Your learned driving and took licence against the command of your Provincial Superior and Council and bought a car which is of a high monetary value, which even the Superior can administer only with the consent of the Council. This is a very grave violation of the vows of obedience and poverty.
4. You have not entrusted your salary [to the congregation] from December 2017. This is a grave violation of the vow of poverty.
5. You published your book *Snehamazhayil,* which your Provincial Superior had asked you not to do but gave you another alternative. Yet you published it—also without the permission of the local hierarch. This is a twofold violation of the vow of obedience.
6. You have made monetary transactions for publishing the book which exceeds the amount, which even the Superior General of the FCC can use for extraordinary expenditure, without any permission. This is a grave infringement of the vows of poverty and obedience [sic].
7. You have published articles in some non-Christian newspapers and weeklies without seeking permission from the Provincial Superior, which are violations of the vow of obedience.

8. You are repeatedly appearing before the social media [sic] and TV channels from 20 September 2018, without the knowledge of your superiors. You are belittling the Catholic Church and FCC making false accusations.
9. You are going out late in the evening and are coming back late at night without permission, which is against the religious discipline of FCC.
10. You are not participating in community prayer, common meals and recreation, which is against the religious principle of FCC.
11. You violated the dress code of FCC in public without any permission.
12. You violated the rule of cloister by keeping a journalist in your room for one night.
13. You caused grave external scandal and harm to the Church and FCC by participating in the protest held by the SOS Action Council on 20 September 2018 at [the] Ernakulam High Court junction and through improper behaviours [sic] in religious life and violations of religious discipline.

You are called upon to give your explanation on the above matter and also why further canonical process shall not be taken against you. You are asked to give your explanation on these charges in writing on or before 6 February 2019.

With love and prayers,
-sd
Sister Ann Joseph FCC
[stamp]

Response of Sister Lucy Kalapura to the First Canonical Warning Issued by Superior General, FCC

Dated: 1 Feb 2019
From:
Sister Lucy Kalapura FCC,
F.C. Convent Vimala Home,
Karackamala P.O.
Mananthawady, Wynad [sic]

To
Sister Ann Joseph, FCC,
Superior General,
Franciscan Clarist Congregation,
Portiuncula, Asokapuram,
Aluva P.O., PIN: 680101

Ref: Your letter issued to me dated 18 January 2019 levelling thirteen allegations

Rev. Sister Superior General,

1. I am humbly submitting the following explanations for the aforesaid letter. My non-appearance before you was not wilful. I was not in the physical and mental condition to travel long distances. As you are aware, I am very much embarrassed and tensed by you cornering me and making untrue and unnecessary allegations against me. On various occasions previously, when I met the superiors of the congregation, I was inhumanly harassed and was even compelled me to kneel down before them. Needless to say, it affects the dignity of any person. I have not made any scandalous statements before the media and didn't try to justify anything as I

am fully convinced that I have not made any mistakes and the ones seen are exaggerated.

2. As you are well aware that I was at the Dwaraka Convent for ten and a half years and came to the present house only few years ago. I was afraid of going to the convent as required in the letter dated 10 May 2015 as I was expecting humiliation at the time.

3. It is true that I have learned driving and obtained a licence. As you are well aware, several nuns of various congregations are driving their own vehicles. Moreover, I am teacher and actively involve [sic] in social issues. Therefore, a vehicle is very much essential for my activities. The car that I use is comparatively cheap in the market. Besides, I have not bought it as a luxury item. So don't take it as a violation of the vows of obedience and poverty. As a teacher for ever so many years, the entire salary, I was giving to the congregation (1993 onwards). Even my request for the release of rupees ten thousand was denied some time ago. I am not spending the money on luxuries or comforts but using it for social purposes.

4. It is true that I have published a book titled *Snehamazhayil*. This book is an anthology of poems mostly based on nature and of 'God's presence'. It is a book that has a spiritual approach emphasizing the importance of love and compassion. It is true that it required some money to publish the book. I think it is for a good cause and has not violated any vows.

5. I humbly feel, it is not appropriate to state that a Christian shall not publish articles in 'non-Christian newspapers and weeklies'. Literature doesn't have communal divides, I feel. There are ever so many Christian writers in Kerala and most of them are writing in non-Christian journals and weeklies. In a pluralistic and secular society like ours, such restrictions are not fair since it is a communally spirited statement also. It is true that I have appeared on TV channels on a few occasions. However, I didn't make any statement belittling the Catholic Church or FCC; nor did I make

any false accusations. I have not lived in 'such a way' as hinted in the notice (Point 9). It is true that I have attended prayer meetings and other social activities. All things were within the limits of a nun's life. I am doing my prayers as a devoted Christian. Actually I am the one being ostracized by the others, including at the time of meals and recreation. I had not 'regularly violated' the dress code of the FCC, but in some situations nuns do wear churidars. When I was sent to attend a course at Bengaluru, the then superior herself had given me two sets of churidars. Moreover, I have various health problems also, while continuously wearing the present dress, especially the polyester materials.

6. A young girl who is a journalist had came [sic] to meet me and it was too late for return and she had to live in the convent in a compelling circumstance.
7. Participating in the protest held by the SOS Action Council on 20 September 2018, I was a part of a great movement organized by various social groups—including womenfolk from the Catholic Church. As you are well aware, the issue was that one Bishop committed rape on a nun. I thought it is essential to support the victim rather than standing with the culprit. Actually, we have to support nuns of the Missionaries of Jesus, especially since we are participating and sharing their house in Indore with them.
8. I have not violated any rules or broke the vows, as you have repeatedly stated in your letter. I am living as a dedicated nun, and I have tried my level best to extend love and compassion to the community and society, especially as a teacher.
9. In the light of the above explanation, I request you not to proceed with punitive action against me as I have not violated any of the Canonical dictums.

Yours faithfully,
Sister Lucy Kalapura

Second Canonical Warning Letter Issued by Superior General, FCC

[FCC letterhead]
Superior General, Portiuncula, FCC Generalate

Prot. No. 61/2019
14 Feb 2019

To,
Sister Lucy Kalapura FCC
FC Convent Vimala Home,
Karackamala P.O. Wayanad
Mananthavady

Sub: Second Canonical Warning Letter (CCEO can. 500 § 2, N. 2) to Sister Lucy Kalapura by Superior General

Dear Sister Lucy Kalapura,

    Having verified a number of violations of the canonical norms and the rules of the Franciscan Clarist Congregation (FCC) on your part during the past years and having verified your refusal to heed to the corrections and admonitions of your legitimate superiors and correct yourself, you were given the first canonical warning on 1 January 2019. In that warning you were asked to meet me personally and eventually present your possible defence. You refused to comply with the instructions contained in that warning letter. Now (1 Feb 2019) you have given your written reply, trying to justify your refusal to meet me, your legitimate Superior General. In your reply, you further refuse to acknowledge your wrongdoings and violations of the canonical norms and rules.

    For all the violations mentioned in the canonical warning, you try to present personal justifications pretending that you have a right to do everything [of your choice]. Even if it is explicitly against the canonical norms and rules of the FCC, you think that is your right. Being a perpetually professed FCC sister for so many years, you should know that through the profession you made freely and willingly, you expressed your readiness to accept and to obey the canonical norms and rules regarding religious life and the rules and regulations of the FCC enshrined in our Constitution. Many of your actions mentioned in the canonical warning go against such norms and rules. Through the vow of poverty, we freely and willingly renounce [sic] to have personal properties and to administer earnings. For spending money, we need the permission of the legitimate superiors. We are also bound to give testimony to the gospel values of humility, suffering and sacrifice, following the example of our Lord who called us to imitate his life.

Your written reply was evaluated by me together with my Council members and I find it insufficient and unacceptable. Instead of providing reasonable and valid explanations according to the spirit of religious life, you are trying to give just your personal justifications. Since your lifestyle and actions are not in line with our religious and community life, through the second canonical warning, you are once more invited to correct yourself and rectify your wrongdoings.

In this second canonical warning, I formally inform you that FCC cannot accept your explanations as satisfactory, since the allegations against you are juridically proven. I repeat here the proven allegations against you:

1. You have not obeyed my order that I gave you as the Superior General on 1 January 2019, to come and meet me in person (*The Rule and Constitution of FCC* N. 16).
2. You did not obey the transfer order dated 10 May 2015 by the Statement of Obedience from your Provincial Superior. This is a grave violation of the vow of obedience.
3. You do not [sic] duly submit your salary to the community from December 2017 onwards. This is a grave violation against the vow

of poverty (CCEO cc. 529 §3; 534 n.1 *Rule and Constitution of FCC N.26*; the *Way of Life of FCC N.27*).

4. You are not regularly participating in community prayer, common meals, and recreation and this is against the religious principle of FCC (CCEO cc. 538 §§1-2; the *Way of Life of FCC N.76, 77*).
5. By buying a personal car, you acted against the legitimate order of your Provincial Superior and the Council. For the amount involved in this deal, even the superiors would have required the consent of the respective council. [sic] This is a very grave violation of the vows of obedience and poverty. (*The Rule and Constitution of FCC* NN. 26, 161, 162).
6. You made monetary transactions in publishing a book and the amount exceeds that which even the Superior General of FCC can use for extraordinary expenditure without permission. This is a grave violation of the vow of poverty (the *Way of Life of FCC N.27, 332*).
7. You published your book *Snehamazhayil* which your Provincial Superior had objected to. This is another example of the violation of vow of obedience by you (CCEO cc. 622 §2; the *Way of Life of FCC N.166*).
8. You are repeatedly appearing before the social media and TV channels and are writing in newspapers and weeklies from 20 September 2018 onwards, without the knowledge and permission of your legitimate superiors (CCEO cc. 660, 662 §2; the *Way of Life of FCC N.166*). Your statements and writings are often one-sided and biased as well as harmful to the image of the Church and its legitimate authority.
9. You are seen going out late in the evening and coming back too late at night without permission which is against the religious discipline of FCC (the *Way of Life of FCC N. 103*).
10. You have violated the dress code of FCC in public (CCEO c. 540; the *Rule and Constitution of FCC N. 101*).

11. You violated the rule of the cloister by keeping a lady journalist in your room for one night (CCEO c. 541; the *Rule and Constitution of FCC N. 59*).

You have also made other serious violations of rules and regulations of FCC which your legitimate superiors have made known to you from time to time. So far, you are not showing any willingness to correct yourself and your explanations show no sign of repentance but only unreasonable and unacceptable self-justification. You are indeed persisting in the above allegations charged against you. These things compel me to proceed with further canonical steps as prescribed by the *Code of Canons of the Eastern Churches* and the Rule and Constitution of the FCC in order to safeguard the religious discipline of the FCC.

Hence, I, the undersigned Sister Ann Joseph FCC, Superior General of the Franciscan Clarist Congregation of which you are [a] perpetually professed member, hereby issue this second canonical warning, inviting you to change your mind and attitude, sincerely, and to reform yourself for living the FCC charism fully in an exemplary manner. If you do not respond to this second canonical warning, expressing in writing your unconditional willingness to reform yourself and to fully abide by the norms of the *Code of Canons of the Eastern Churches* and the *Rule and Constitution* and *Way of Life of the FCC (Proper Law)*, I am afraid, I will be constrained to proceed with your dismissal from the Franciscan Clarist Congregation. You have the right under the Canon Law and Proper Law of FCC to self-defence, including a canonical counsel in this matter at all stages.

I do expect a positive reply from you, with unconditional declaration in writing of your compliance with the instructions of your legitimate Superior, on or before 10 of March 2019. If no reply reaches me within that date, I shall take it as your declaration of unwillingness to comply with my instructions, and I may have to proceed further, as indicated above.

I earnestly ask you once again to reflect on the precious gift of your religious vocation, realize your mistakes, and rectify your wrong attitudes and doings by making the correct reparations and complying fully with the *Rule and Constitution of FCC* and *Way of Life of the FCC*.

May the Holy Spirit guide you in taking the right decision.

Yours in Our Lord,
-sd   -sd
Sister Ann Joseph FCC   Sister Filby FCC
                            Notary/Secretary to the General Council

[stamp]
[FCC stamp]

Response Given by Sister Lucy Kalapura to Superior General FCC

From:
Sister Lucy Kalapura FCC,
F.C. Convent Vimala Home,
Karackamala P.O.
Mananthawady, Wynad [sic]

To
Sister Ann Joseph, FCC,
Superior General,
Franciscan Clarist Congregation,
Portiuncula, Asokapuram,
Aluva P.O., PIN: 680101

Ref: **Reply to letters dated 1 Jan 2019, 18 Jan 2019, 14 Feb 2019, 4 March 2019**

Reverend Sister Ann Joseph,

1. It was the duty of [the] FCC to participate in the fight for justice by the six sisters of Missionaries of Jesus following the continued

sexual abuse of one of the sisters by Bishop Franco. (Rule N. 80). But [the] FCC maintained complete silence. God had selected Sister Lucy Kalapura FCC for this mission. Acknowledge and recognize the same and, till the conclusion of the legal action, support and encourage the six sisters alienated by the Missionaries of Jesus congregation—that should be our mission.

Responses

The *Rule and Constitution of FCC* and the *Way of Life of FCC.*

In Rule N. 58

'Brotherhood should not be confined only to our community; it must be propagated to the world around us.'

In Rule N. 71

'With our believers' vision, we must be capable of finding God's design in the markers of Time. It is imperative that in our monastic community transformations and acculturation take place following the changes in the culture of the society we live in. Through prayers and motivation, society should always show the sincerity to help the sisters who are engaged in apostolic activities.

In Rule N. 80

'The happiness, hopes, sorrows and anxieties of humans of this day, especially the poor and the downtrodden should be ours too. Therefore, we must approach our brethren who are in pain with compassionate hearts, render them our loving service and act as Good Samaritans.'

2. The book *Snehamazhayil* was published after an unbroken, long three-year wait (the *Way of Life of FCC14, 165*; the *Rule and*

Constitution of FCC N. 86). It was [with] God's will and blessings that articles got written in non-Christian newspapers, appearances were made on visual media [and] the lyrics for the devotional CD '*Devalayam*' were composed.

Responses

In Rule N. 86

'Promotion of arts, literature, and cultural activities should be seen as apostolic work. St. Francis Assisi was a peerless poet and artist. Sisters who have an interest in literature, music and other arts should be encouraged and inspired to write poems, articles and books. Using printed materials, cinema, plays, radio, television and all media, Christ's gospel should be spread all over the world.'

In Rule N. 61

'Beholding the glory and presence of God in all Nature, we are bounden to love it.'

In Rule N. 105

'Superiors shall listen with compassionate hearts to sisters and motivate them to make contribute personally to the welfare of the Holy See and the society.'

In Rule N. 60

'We must strive to discover God's greatness, knowledge and love in all scientific progress, inventions, arts and cultures.'

3. After working in a private school from 1993 and in a government school from December 1996, and after requesting for permission

from the congregation which has been receiving my salary and other benefits in full every month, I am using a car for my convenience to visit the houses of my students who are in strife and engage with full social commitment.

Responses

In Rule N. 81

'In that manner, education also aims at the progress of the community, of which a man is a member, and for which as a young man he will need to take on responsibility. We must engage in educational activities with a broad vision, enthusiasm and dedication. To be productive, mental skills and qualities of the heart, high-level planning, a mind ready to reform and adapt are needed.'

4. In the circumstances where one faces much health problems from the torrid heat, one waits for sanction after seeking permission to wear cotton churidar-kameezes.

Responses

In Rule N. 101

'The monastic habit must be simple, humble and, at the same time, appropriate and universal. It must promote health, suitable for the time and place, and facilitate the service to be rendered by the wearers.'

In Rule N. 11

'Our congregation is a part of the worldwide Franciscan family. At the same time, we have our own identity. We must formulate and regulate our activities considering the special circumstances of our nation and its needs.'

5. The foundation of all Christian laws is the Gospel. Without that, the monastic laws, which go by the letter, will outdo even the civil laws.

In Rule N. 18

'In all lawful and reasonable matters, we are bound to obey the political rulers and the civil laws.'

I am taking another step now with the same determination and fervidity with which I took the first step to become a nun in 1982. For the rest of my life, I have readied myself to live as Sister Lucy Kalapura, to live a genuine monastic life in true spirituality, to spurn mercilessly sham spirituality, and to be the voice of those who have been denied justice and silenced in the Church and society.

After having celebrated monasticism by living in happy spirituality and remaining unperturbed by any adversity, I must live my life in an uplifting manner. I came into monastery as a free spirit, of my own will, and to live for the community's poor, friendless and those denied justice and thus enjoy my religiosity. I aspire with all my heart to live an even more elevated life in [the] FCC, using all my God-given talent and creativity to this end. In anticipation of all your blessings,

Affectionately yours,
-sd
Sister Lucy Kalapura
Date: 10 March 2019

Letter of Expulsion from the FCC

[FCC letterhead]
Superior General, Portiuncula, FCC Generalate
**Decree of Dismissal of Sister Lucy Kalapura FCC from the Franciscan Clarist Congregation
According to CCEO c.553 and 500 and FCC Constitutions, article no. 103**

I. Facts of the Case *(factispecies)*

1. Sister Lucy Kalapura FCC, born on 6 June 1965 at Karikottakary [sic] in Kerala joined the Franciscan Clarist Congregation after her twelve years of schooling as a candidate on 24 June 1982 and made her first profession of religious vows in the same congregation on 22 May 1985 and her final profession on 21 May 1991. After her first profession, she was sent for university studies by the FCC and she successfully completed her BSc degree and Bachelors [sic] of Education (BEd) and after her few [sic] years of teaching ministry in north India, the FCC managed to get a teaching post for her in a Government-aided Catholic Management school at Dwaraka in Wayanad. While teaching in the school, she was transferred among various neighbouring FCC convents and since 2016, she is a member of FCC Convent, Vimala House, Karakkamala, Wayanad Dt., Kerala, India.

2. Her life as a religious [person] in the Franciscan Clarist Congregation was marked by small to big problems at various stages of her life. On 30 August 2003, her then Provincial Superior warned her in writing for [the] physical violence that she inflicted on another sister of her community while she was the local superior of the community. On 10 May 2015, the then Provincial Superior issued a transfer order to her from FCC Convent Kommayad to FCC Convent Dwaraka. But Sister Lucy refused to obey the transfer order and remained in the

same community. On 29 April 2017, Sister Lucy Kalapura petitioned the Provincial Superior [for] a financial help of fifteen thousand rupees for a member of her family. The Provincial Superior replied asking for the name of the person and [for the] details and purpose of the request, to which Sister Lucy did not reply at all. Thereafter, Sister Lucy sent an undated letter to the Provincial Superior asking for permission to learn driving two-wheeler and four-wheeler vehicles and on 3 June 2017, the Provincial Superior informed her that permission could not be granted.

3. On 25 November 2017, Sister Lucy Kalapura requested the Provincial Superior's permission to publish the poems she wrote as a book and for a letter of recommendation from the Provincial and a grant of fifty thousand rupees towards [the] publishing of the book. On the same day, the Provincial informed her that the permission to publish the book could not be sanctioned as the permission of the Bishop of the place was needed to publish books. At the same time, the Provincial suggested her to publish [sic] those poems first in the journal of the Congregation, namely in *Vachanamrutam* and *Snehadeepthi*. In December 2017, Sister Lucy stopped handing over her salary from the school to the FCC. Later, on 3 January 2018, the Provincial Superior asked Sister Lucy to submit a hard copy of her poems so that it could be assessed by experts to see whether it is worth publishing them as a book. Sister Lucy, however, did not heed to [sic] this instruction and [take on board the] suggestion of the Provincial Superior and, without the needed [sic] permission, published her collection of poems as a book entitled *Snehamazhayil* in February 2018, and on 10 March 2018 [she] sent a WhatsApp message to the Provincial Superior informing her that the book was already published and it costed [sic] fifty thousand rupees. Likewise, she published a CD containing Christian devotional hymns under the title '*Devalayam*' during the same period without any permission from the FCC or the local hierarch.

4. The Provincial Superior, on 13 March 2018, in her letter (Prot. 16/2018) highlighted these violations and acts of disobedience and asked for explanations from Sister Lucy Kalapura and instructed her to submit the reply within a week. However, Sister Lucy Kalapura did not respond to that letter. Hence on 28 March 2018, the Provincial Superior again sent a letter (Prot. 18/2018) reminding her to reply to her letter dated 13 March 2018 and informed her that any further failure to respond to that letter might result in legal steps against her. On 4 April 2018, Sister Lucy Kalapura replied stating that the allegations in the letter dated 13 March 2018 were baseless and that she considered such letters as instruments to torture her mentally. Further, she stated thus: 'I must live my faith, my ideal, my conviction. Therefore, as it is indicated in the letters I got, for having done good, for the proclamation of the Word, and if you find me not suitable for you, you can take any decision. But you must arrange facilities for me to live quietly. For that, I should get compensation for the service which I rendered in the past thirty-two years. For the work I did in the school for the past twenty-five years, I should get remuneration too.' On 19 May 2018, Sister Stephina FCC, the Provincial, wrote a letter (Prot. 31/2018) of warning about the deliberate and frequent violation of the proper law of the FCC by Sister Lucy Kalapura and warning her of initiating dismissal procedure against her if she failed to correct her lifestyle.

5. On 28 May 2018, Sister Lucy petitioned to her Provincial team to permit her to buy a car. On 4 June 2018, [the] Provincial, Sister Stephina FCC, through her letter (Prot. No. 32/2018) replied that the petition was discussed in the Provincial Council held on 2 June 2019 [sic], and that the Council decided not to grant such permission as it was the policy of the Province not to have a vehicle even for the common purposes in the Province, because in the area of the Province, ownership of a vehicle was considered a luxury and that Franciscan sisters should be very careful to lead a life that shuns away [sic] from any form of luxury. The Provincial

reminded Sister Lucy that the practice of all sisters of the Province was to use public transport for travel or take an autorickshaw to visit families etc. where buses are not available. Despite such a clear rejection of the requested permission, having given the reasons, Sister Lucy bought a car and got it registered on 28 July 2018 with her name as Sister Lucy K.S. and without giving her address and got the Reg. Number [sic] KL-12-L-9719 for her car.

6. Thereafter, her life in the local community was marked by frequent unlawful absence[s]. She was seen many times in Television shows [sic], and a lot of write-up [sic] appeared in the media by her and about her. Many a time, she went out of the community without the permission, either informing the Superior or without it, and came back to the convent late in the evening or even near to or after midnight, and the Superior of the convent had to be awake to let her in when she came back. During the same period, she posted her photo in the Facebook [sic] in secular dress and started criticizing the religious habit of the FCC in her TV shows and in her write-ups. Moreover, one time she brought a journalist, whom she met in her life for the first time [sic], into the convent and shared her room with the journalist during one whole night [sic], without any kind of permission. In fact, she could have availed of the guest room of the convent, had she asked for the permission of her Superior. This created a lot of fear and anxiety in the minds of [the] other sisters of the convent. They started living with the constant fear Sister Lucy Kalapura could bring into the convent any one at any time [sic] and that there might be strangers or activists or journalists within the enclosure of the convent even at night.

7. On 20 November 2018, Rev. Sister Ann Joseph FCC, the Superior General of the FCC, through her letter Prot. No. 402/2018 asked [sic] explanation from Sister Stephina FCC, the Provincial Superior of the St. Mary's Province, Mananthavady, regarding Sister Lucy Kalapura, as the media [had] reported a lot about Sister Lucy Kalapura. After that, the Superior General, on 28 November 2018, telephoned Sister

Lucy and asked Sister Lucy to meet the Superior General in person. Since Sister Lucy did not give any date on which she was ready to meet the Superior General, on 12 December 2019 [sic] in writing directed Sister Lucy to inform the Superior General in writing on which day Sister Lucy would be ready to meet the Superior General. On 16 December 2018, Sister Lucy replied to that letter in writing, but without a date for the demanded meeting. Therefore, on 1 January 2019, Sister Ann Joseph FCC, the Superior General, issued Sister Lucy Kalapura the first canonical warning with the threat of dismissal from the FCC. In the same warning letter, Sister Lucy was instructed to meet the Superior General in person on 9 January 2019 and to explain her reasons for the continuous disobedience. However, Sister Lucy did not appear before the Superior General on the stipulated date and time. But on 8 January she wrote to the Superior General informing her that because of the general strike announced [sic] to be held on that date, she would not be able to come to meet her. The Superior General then informed Sister Lucy that she should appear before her on any date between 11–14 January 2019, after informing her about the date and the time of arrival. However, Sister Lucy did not reply to this letter. Hence on 18 January 2019, the Superior General wrote another letter to Sister Lucy Kalapura (Prot. 12/2019) reiterating the allegations in the first canonical warning and making her aware of her grave and persistent disobedience in which she continues by refusing to meet the Superior General. On 1 February 2019, Sister Lucy replied to that letter of the Superior General, in which she attempted to defend herself against the thirteen allegations levelled against her in the letter of the Superior General.

8. Since the explanations given by Sister Lucy Kalapura were not satisfactory, and since Sister Lucy did not amend her ways in the meantime, the Superior General, on 14 February 2019, through her letter Prot. No. 61/2019 issued the second canonical warning to Sister Lucy Kalapura. On 1 March 2019, Sister Lucy Kalapura wrote

an email to Sister Ann Joseph, the Superior General, requesting permission to wear 'salwar–kameez' instead of the FCC habit and veil due to health reasons and informing her that 'as per the doctor's advice' her health condition was not suited to wear habit and veil [sic] and that she needed an appointment to explain her situation in that regard and show the Superior General 'the doctor's certificate' regarding it. On 4 March 2019, Sister Ann Joseph replied to Sister Lucy giving her [an] appointment on 11 March 2019 to meet her at the Generalate in her office at 11 a.m. In that letter, the Superior General informed Sister Lucy that her request not to take any decision on her request to wear 'salwar–kameez' before hearing her was granted, and assured her in the following words, 'As I have written in 3.5, after I have received the doctor's certificate and after hearing you in person, I, with the help of my Council, will consider your petition regarding the religious habit.' To this letter, Sister Lucy Kalapura replied through an email to the Superior General on 5 March 2019 which contained the following sentences: 'When it is too cold, the FCC sisters wear Jacket, [sic] shawl and other types of woolen [sic] clothes. Likewise when it is too hot, there should be freedom to prevent it. From the letter I understood that your permission is like a document written on water. You[r] hard heart is kept in the laws [sic]. The foundation of all laws in the Church is the Gospel. That is foreign to you. Sorry, as I compelled by my body, I wear [sic] churidar till rainy season.' On 6 March 2019, Sister Lucy Kalapura wrote to the Superior General another consolidated defence against the allegations levelled against her in the First Canonical Warning dated 1 January 2019, and the ensuing letter of 18 January 2019, the Second Canonical Warning of 14 February 2019 and the reply of the Superior General on 4 March 2019, regarding her request to wear [a] salwar–kameez instead of the FCC religious habit.

9. On 10 March 2019, in the evening Sister Lucy Kalapura wrote another email to the Superior General demanding her to change the

venue of the meeting [sic] from the office of the Superior General as she was 'frightened to come inside' the Generalate and suggesting that the meeting 'can be at the parish church publicly' to which the Superior General did not respond as she saw that email only after 10 a.m. on the following day. On 11 March 2019, Sister Lucy arrived at the FCC Generalate accompanied of [sic] a layman and a big crew of various TV Channels in many vehicles. First she refused to enter the Generalate, insisting that the meeting should take place outside the Generalate. When she realized it would not happen, then she agreed to enter the Generalate and to meet the Superior General in her office, provided she would be accompanied by a lady police officer, which was permitted. Thus in the presence of the lady police officer, Sister Lucy met the Superior General in her office. When Sister Lucy was asked to submit the Doctor's [sic] certificate regarding her inability to wear the habit of the FCC, Sister Lucy replied that she did not take [sic] it with her. When she was asked whether she had any explanations or defence to offer against the allegations levelled against her, she replied that there was nothing to add to her defence other than what she wrote in her replies to the canonical warning letters. Since the lady police officer was witnessing to [sic] all these in the office, the Superior General did not repeat the allegations against her and concluded the session with a short prayer.

10. Since the consolidated defence letter of Sister Lucy was not deemed satisfactory nor [seemed to be] addressing the allegations against her, Sister Ann Joseph FCC, the Superior General, with the consent of her Council, on 12 March 2019 (Prot. No. 136/2109) issued a detailed eighteen-page long Show Cause Notice to Sister Lucy Kalapura FCC, explaining in detail why her actions were being considered as [sic] deliberate violation of the vows of obedience and poverty and that her actions were serious violations of the Proper Law of FCC for which she could be dismissed unless she gave satisfactory explanation and unless there would be sufficient reform in her behaviour. As in the case of the previous two canonical

warning letters, this Show-Cause Notice also ended up in the TV Channels which spoke to her [sic]. But unlike the previous canonical warning letters, which were uploaded in the internet [sic], the Show Cause Notice was not seen uploaded in the [sic] electronic media. On 13 April 2019, Sister Lucy Kalapura replied to the Show Cause in writing, offering her defence and referring to her earlier defence letters. Even after the Show Cause Notice, Sister Lucy continued to be active in [sic] her Facebook account, even criticizing the FCC and the Catholic Church at large under various pretexts and continued to make journeys without due permission even for many days at a stretch, and was away from the community even during the Holy Week, and once [sic] telephoned her local superior informing [sic] that she would be coming back to the convent after midnight around 1.30 a.m. The local Superior had to be awake to open the door and let her in. However, Sister Lucy reached back [sic] the convent only around 4.30 a.m. and the Superior of the community had to be awake waiting for her till then.

II. The Law (*In Iure*)

A: Fundamental Principles

11. Each human being has got different levels of existence. First and foremost, as a human person, there are fundamental human rights which no external authority can take away. Then by virtue of baptism or by virtue of joining the Catholic Church, a Christian faithful has got rights and reciprocal duties in the Catholic Church. To have those rights, the Christian faithful must follow the laws of the Catholic Church. Here itself, certain restrictions have already come to bind the Christian faithful like the fundamental right to believe in 'any' religion and to propagate 'any' religion. By accepting the Catholic Church as his/her religion, in this context, the Christian faithful forfeits his/her right to profess any religion,

since he/she has already bound himself/herself to a religion. It is an [sic] analogous to a person getting married. Before getting married, a person has the fundamental right to marry any person who is legally not bound by another marriage bond. But, once a person enters a valid marriage, as long as the marriage lasts, the person is not free to marry again. His/her rights about marriage and family relationship are conditioned by obligations undertaken by [the parties of] that marriage. He/she cannot simply argue based on the [sic] fundamental human rights that I have the right and freedom to share my love and life with anyone of my choice. Likewise, before joining a religious congregation of the Catholic Church there are many rights enjoyed by a [sic] Christian faithful. But by joining the religious institute, many of such rights are restricted to [sic] that person as long as that person continues in that religious institute.

12. Nobody has an innate right to be a member of [the] FCC. The membership in the FCC is contingent on the faithful observance of the religious vows made in [the] Franciscan Clarist Congregation. In the religious profession, which one makes freely and knowingly, after many of formation, one takes the vows of obedience, chastity and poverty to be observed according to the Proper Law of FCC, which includes the Constitutions of the FCC (*The Rule and Constitution of the Franciscan Clarist Congregation*) and the General Directory (*The Way of Life of Franciscan Clarist Congregation*). The membership in the FCC based on the vow to live according to the Proper Law of the FCC. One makes the profession of vows and obedience, chastity and poverty not in the abstract, [and one may] not [be permitted] to interpret and observe [them] according to one's whims and fancies, but in the FCC, which is a religious congregation in Syro-Malabar Church, which is one of the Oriental Catholic Churches that is governed by the Code of Canons of the Eastern Churches (CCEO). Nobody compels anyone to join this religious congregation. It is always one's desire based on the divine

call one receives from Jesus Christ, the Divine Master, and then one makes the religious profession in it, first temporarily and after many years of living that religious life, upon request, one is permitted to make the perpetual profession of religious vows. 'A vow is a deliberate and free promise made to God concerning a possible and better good; the virtue of religion requires that it be fulfilled.' (CCEO c. 889). The vows of obedience, chastity and poverty which thus a member freely takes are not private vows, but public, because such a religious profession is accepted in the name of Church by a legitimate ecclesiastical superior from the FCC. Thus one becomes a religious sister belonging to the FCC, a *sanyasini* (to use the terminology dear to [the] Indian Ethos), a person who decided to lead a life according to charism, spirituality and Proper Law [sic] of the FCC. Even in the age-old Indian Tradition, a *sanyasini* doses [sic] not wear any dress, but only a religious habit.

13. Life in the FCC is not something optional for a person who makes [a] religious profession in it. Once a person becomes a member in it, [from] that time onwards life according to its Proper Law becomes obligatory. A member of the FCC must live her religious [sic] not in the abstract but in the concrete lifestyle of the Congregation, according to the spirituality and charism of it, defined and protected by its Proper Law. The moment one is convinced that she is not called to this life as a religious in the FCC, there is the possibility of leaving it. When there is moral certainty achieved after repeated warning and correction that a member is not leading and is not suited for life in the FCC, the competent authority, namely the Superior General with the consent of her Council, can also dismiss such a member from the Congregation.

14. If one wishes only to preach the Gospel of Christ and do evangelization according to one's own whims and fancies, that person can do that. There is no need for her to join the FCC. The Franciscan Clarist Congregation is a religious Congregation, and it means that its members live [sic] Christian life as a separate and

unique state of life, which is not like other states of life recognized by [sic] Canon of Law of the Catholic Church, namely the lay state or clerical state. The essential elements of religious life include the practice of the evangelical counsels of chastity, poverty and obedience to be observed according to the proper law of the Congregation and community life under a local superior in a local community. As religious life is a life of renunciation and detachment from the world, to denote it, one is to observe the law regarding enclosure and religious habit. The vow of obedience obliges every FCC to obey the legitimate directives of one's lawful superiors within the FCC, namely, the local superior, the Provincial Superior and the Superior General. The Roman Pontiff also comes under the category of internal superior of the FCC, as the Supreme Authority of the Catholic Church. The vow of obedience makes it imperative to its members to ask permission from the competent authority for everything that is not daily routine or where the proper law of the Congregation or the custom within the Congregation stipulates so. The vow of poverty obliges a sister of the FCC not to have a [sic] free use of money and to use temporal goods only with proper permission and avoiding all elements of luxury. Hence, if a person wants to have free use of one's property or salary, it is not possible as long as that person is a member of a religious institute [sic].

15. Before the Indian civil law, the [sic] membership in the FCC is considered only as a [sic] membership in a private organization governed by its bylaws and thus is governed by the norms regarding private contract, since India, as a secular country, does not legislate on religious matters. Each religion and each denomination has the right to govern itself according to its own personal laws and bylaws, and as long as these laws do not violate the established norms of the State and as long as there are no human right violations, the judiciary of India will be evaluating even the dismissal procedure of a member by evaluating whether the rules and bylaws governing the private organization are respected in the process.

16. Once a person is a member of any organization, that person is obliged to follow the bylaws and norms governing that organization. After joining a school a student cannot say that I will not wear the uniform of that school. He/she will be thrown out of that school. After joining the Indian Administrative Service or Indian Police Service, one cannot say that whenever I like I will publish books or join a TV channel discussion. There are norms that stipulate asking and receiving proper permissions to do that which bind them all. Even political parties sometime[s] insist that without the permission of the proper authority, its members should not join a TV channel discussion. If that is the case, how much more important it is for the religious sister who renounced the world and who took the vow of obedience and thus make [sic] a promise to GOD to obey the Constitutions and Directory of the Congregation, to obey the norms regarding the religious habit and the norms regarding asking and receiving permissions from the competent authority where ever [sic] the proper law stipulated so.
17. If the law stipulates that one must ask [sic] permission to do something, it means that asking of permission in itself is not enough and if the request is denied, then one cannot proceed as if he/she got permission to act in the given case. If the law demands that one should ask permission, the implication is that one is permitted to act only if the needed [sic] permissions is sanctioned. If the asked permission [sic] is denied then there are only two options: either to go to the higher authorities and make a recourse against the decision, or to accept the decision of the authority which denied the requested permission.

B: The Law Proper

18. The supreme authority of the Catholic Church is exercised ordinarily by the Roman Pontiff and extra-ordinarily [sic] in the ecumenical council. The Second Vatican Council, which was the last ecumenical council through its decree *Perfectae Caritatis* (hereafter PC) taught

authentically and authoritatively on [sic] the nature of religious life of religious life and religious vows. PC teaches thus:

Through the vow of obedience a religious surrender to God in self-sacrifice the free determination of their lives ... they accept the leadership of the superiors in the service of Christ's whole body, even as Christ served his brothers and sisters in obedience to his Father and laid down his life as a ransom [sic] for many (see Mt. 20, 28; Jn 10, 14–18) ... [The r]eligious trust and court God's will; they obey their superiors, therefore, in humility and under the direction of constitutions and rules. They surrender their minds and hearts, their gifts of nature and grace in doing what they are told, in living a life under [sic] obedience.

FCC Constitutions' Art. 14 stipulates thus: 'The vow of obedience is a conscious surrender of one's free will to God, promising to be obedient to the [relevant] legal superiors and to the rules of the Congregation, in order to be able to unite oneself to the salvific will of God in a stabler and more secure manner, this is done by [sic] the inspiration of Jesus Christ who became obedient till death on the cross.' Article 16 of the same Constitution states: 'Under the influence of the Holy Spirit, the religious must subject themselves in faith to their superiors who hold the place of God. Our obedience in faith should be humble, generous, responsible and free. We are bound to obey our superiors in all things except what is sinful. Sisters should use both the force of their intellect and will, and gifts of nature and grace, to execute the commands and to fulfil the duties entrusted to them. In case the sisters find it difficult to conform to the decisions of the superiors, they can humbly report to the superiors their own ideas for the common good. But the final decision lies with the superior ...'

19. The FCC is part of the Franciscan family which gives very great importance on the vow of poverty after the example of St. Francis of Assisi and St. Clare. The Second Vatican Council, through its

decree *Perfectae Caritatis* no. 13 teaches thus regarding the vow of poverty: 'Religious must sedulously practice the poverty they have freely chosen as a sign—one in high favour today—of the presence of Christ they imitate.' Regarding the vow of poverty, FCC Constitutions have legislated in detail; FCC Constitutions, Art. 23 stipulates that:

The vow of poverty is the total consecration of oneself to God, by renouncing the right of possession of all things of monetary value and their free use, in order to share our personal talents and charisms for the greater glory of God and the service of mankind, inspired by the example of Christ who, though he was rich in all things, became poor, so that by His poverty, we might become rich.

Article 26 of the same Constitutions states the following:

By the vow of poverty, sisters renounce the free use and administration of things of monetary value. After temporary profession, whatever a sister acquires or receives is the property of Congregation. The members should be satisfied with [the] economic plans made by the Congregation.

Likewise the General Directory of the FCC also have [sic] detailed norms regarding the vow of poverty which bind [sic] every member of the Congregation. The General Directory, which is entitled *The Way of Life of Franciscan Clarist Congregation*, stipulates thus in article 23:

Without the superior's permission, we should not receive or give gifts or exchange, lend or borrow money or things or take charge or leave or leave others in charge of land or properties. But it is permissible to exchange gifts of small value when necessity or courtesy requires it. In matters of food, clothing, treatment, articles of daily use and living rooms, we must follow common life.

Again, in article 25 of *The Way of Life*, we read:

> It is an essential part of [the] spirit of poverty to be simple and moderate in our life. We will become genuine children of St. Francis only if we can maintain the mentality to say 'enough', 'no', regarding temporal things. We must be satisfied with what is necessary for our life and apostolate. Our standard of living should be that of an ordinary man. We must be ready to help the poor by limiting our needs, working hard and bearing the pinches [sic] of poverty.

The Way of Life article 27 legislates thus:

> Sisters including superiors must be strict in monetary matters. Unless compelled by one's office, a sister should not have anything to do with money transactions. **Any money received as payment for work or as personal gift or donation should be entrusted with [sic] the superior, to be included in the common fund.**

Moreover, article 30 of *The Way of Life* stipulates:

> We have to bear witness to poverty as a community also. The local Synaxis must [sic] find way for achieving it. We must experience the pangs of poverty with the poor of the locality and share what we have with them. Experiencing hunger is part of the poverty which we have accepted voluntarily. The time and method of experiencing this should be decided by each community …

20. The Second Vatican Council in its decree *Perfectae Caritatis* no. 16 stipulates that nuns must keep enclosure imposed by their constitutions. Likewise PC 17 teaches that the religious habit is the outward sign of consecration. FCC Constitution's article no. 59 stipulates:

In order to safeguard religious life and the spirit of prayer and recollection, enclosure should be observed in our houses. **No one is allowed to enter the bedrooms of our sisters.** When it is essential, the superiors can prudently permit outsiders to enter the enclosure. Sisters may go on a journey only for a reasonable cause and with the permission of the superior.

Article 103 of *The Way of Life* stipulates:

Sisters should travel only with the permission of the superior. Before going for and after returning from a journey, sisters must meet the superior and inform her the details of the same. Before and after the journey, we must pay a visit to the Blessed Sacrament. When we go to other convents, we must meet the superior first. As far as possible, there must be a companion for the journey. On certain occasions, the superior can permit the sisters to travel alone. Yet there must be a sister companion when a sister goes to a hospital, government offices, shops, [the] bishop's house and [the] presbytery. Only after Holy Mass should sisters go for a journey. **They must be back before Angelus in the evening**. While travelling we must bear witness to our religious spirit in our talk and our dealings and must keep up the spirit of prayer.

Regarding [the] religious habit, article 101 of the Constitution legislates the following:

Our religious habit is a sign of consecration. It should be simple and modest, ordinary, and at the same time, becoming. Moreover it must be in keeping with the requirements of health and must be suited to the times and place and to the needs of the apostolate. All the sisters are expected to wear the religious habit prescribed in our Franciscan Directory. The cord, a Franciscan symbol, should be included in our religious habit.

Regarding the religious habit, we read the following in *The Way of Life* no. 196:

There are two types of habit[s] in the Congregation. A. Habit, scapular, cord, toque, veil. B. Habit, cape, cord, cap, veil. Sisters must wear a rosary on the cord and crucifix at the neck. We can wear white, brown or [an] ash habit. Our habit must bear witness to our religious spirit and modesty. Juniors wear white veils, while seniors wear black veils.

21. *The Code of Canons of the Eastern Churches*, canons 659, 650, and 662 give us the norms regarding the publishing. CCEO c.660 stipulates:

Unless there is a just and reasonable cause, the Christian faithful may not write anything in newspapers, magazines, or periodicals that are wont to attack openly the Catholic religion or good morals; clerics and members of religious institutes [sic] moreover need the permission of those referred to in can. 662.

The Way of Life article 166 stipulates:

The Local Hierarch's permission is required to publish books. To publish articles in newspapers and magazines of non-Christians, the permission of the Provincial Superior is necessary. With the local superior's permission, articles can be published in Catholic magazines.

22. One of the essential elements of religious life is life in the community. CCEO c.410 defines religious life thus:

The religious state is a stable manner of **living in common** in an institute [sic] approved by the Church, by which the Christian faithful, more closely following Christ, Teacher and Exemplar of Holiness, are consecrated by a new and special title through the public vows of obedience, chastity, and poverty observed in accord with the norm of the statutes under a legitimate superior, renounce the world, and totally dedicate themselves to the attainment of perfect charity in the service of the Kingdom of God and the salvation of the world as a sign of the foretelling of heavenly glory.

How to live this community life in [the] FCC is further legislated in the FCC Constitutions and *The Way of Life*. Article 57 of the Constitution stipulates, in addition to the community prayer, community meals and community recreation as means to foster sisterly love and communion in the community and directs every sister to participate daily in these community activities.

23. The 27th Synod of the Syro-Malabar Church held at Kakkanad from 7–18 January 2019 decided that priests and religious may participate in the TV channel discussions and interviews **only with the permission of the respective eparchial bishop or major superior.** This was communicated to the members of the Syro-Malabar Church through the circular of Major Archbishop Cardinal George Alencherry (Prot. No. 0127/2019) dated 18 January 2019 in all Syro-Malabar churches and Eucharistic centres where the Eucharistic celebration takes place on Sundays. The same circular

informed us that the Synod instructed the eparchial bishops and major superiors to give show cause notices to those who commit serious acts of disobedience and to take disciplinary actions against those who do not provide satisfactory replies.

24. The FCC Constitution's article 103 stipulates thus:

A sister who is perpetually professed can be dismissed from the Congregation in the following manner:

i. The reason for dismissal must be grave, culpable and juridically proven, and there is a lack of reform.
ii. Before dismissal two warning[s] were given with the formal threat of dismissal which did not produce any result.
iii. Reasons for dismissal must be presented in writing to the sister, granting her after each warning, full opportunity for defence.
iv. A period of two months must be made available to the sister after the last warning.
v. The Superior General with the consent of her Council is competent to issue a decree of dismissal.
vi. The decree of dismissal cannot be executed unless it is approved by competent authority (Apostolic See/Major Archbishop).

25. CCEO c.503 stipulates thus:

§1. One who leaves the monastery legitimately or has been dismissed from it legitimately can request nothing from the monastery for any work done in it. §2. Nevertheless, the institute [sic] is to observe equity and charity toward a member who is separated from it.

The same law is reiterated in article 103 of FCC Constitutions:

> A Sister who lawfully departs or was lawfully dismissed from the Congregation cannot claim anything from it for any kind

of work performed there. The Congregation, however, shall extend equitable and evangelical charity towards a member who is being separated from it.

III. The Application of the Law (*In Facto*):

26. The Show Cause Notice issued by the Superior General of the Franciscan Clarist Congregation on 12 March 2019 systematically presented the allegations and proofs against Sister Lucy Kalapura FCC. There were seven allegations enumerated in that letter. They are the following:

   26.1 Sister Lucy Kalapura FCC has consciously and wilfully violated the vow of poverty repeatedly and on grave matters:

   26.1.1 Sister Lucy stopped handing over her monthly salary from her job as a schoolteacher to the FCC Congregation [sic] since December 2017.

   26.1.2 Sister Lucy bought a car in her own name, though her request to buy it was rejected by her Provincial.

   26.1.3 Sister Lucy published a book without the needed [sic] permission and by spending fifty thousand rupees. [sic]

   26.2 Sister Lucy Kalapura violated the vow of obedience wilfully and repeatedly and continue to live in her disobedience.

   26.2.1 Sister Lucy disobeyed the order of the Superior General to meet her in person.

   26.2.2 Sister Lucy disobeyed the transfer order given to her in 2015.

   26.2.3 Despite the clear rejection of the sought permission [sic] to learn driving and buying [sic] a vehicle, Sister Lucy in obstinate disobedience learned driving and bought a car.

   26.3 Sister Lucy has violated the proper law of the FCC regarding enclosure and travel.

   26.3.1 Sister Lucy kept a lay person in her bedroom overnight.

26.3.2 Sister Lucy goes out from the convent without asking and receiving permission from her from her [sic] local superior and comes back sometimes very late and at times does not even come back overnight, even without informing [the authorities] about her travel plans and whereabouts and with whom or for what she makes such travels.

26.4 Sister Lucy violated the proper law of the FCC regarding [the wearing of a] religious habit by publishing her photo in the electronic media in lay dress and in travelling in lay dress.

26.5 Sister Lucy violated the canonical norm and the proper law of the FCC regarding [the] publishing of books and articles.

26.6 Sister Lucy violated the norm of the Syro-Malabar Church regarding participation in TV channel programmes and in [relation to] giving interviews.

26.7 Sister Lucy repeatedly violated the norms of the FCC regarding community life, like community prayer, community meals and community recreation.

27. In her reply to the allegations, dated 13 April 2019, Sister Lucy Kalapura FCC rejected all the allegations as intentionally fabricated and as lies and concluded her letter by stating the following: 'Therefore, the Congregation should stop all false allegations against me, and recognizing the good in me, should create an environment in which I can complete my religious life happily.' Regarding most of the allegations, she replied in the above letter that she had responded to them in her earlier defences. Regarding the wearing of secular dress she wrote thus: 'The rejection of my petition dated 1 March 2019 mercilessly (4 March 2019) gives me mental and physical difficulties that the Congregation does not understand my physical difficulties as a member of a religious Congregation.' This assertion that the petition of Sister Lucy Kalapura to wear a Salwar Kameez [sic] was 'mercilessly rejected' in the letter of 4 March 2019, by the

Superior General is far from true. That letter concluded by stating that after having heard Sister Lucy Kalapura in person and after having seen the doctor's certificate regarding the health reasons, the petition could be decided. In that reply, the Superior General also wrote that the Proper Law of the FCC does not require the use of polyester material for the habit and veil and she could have the habit made up [sic] of cotton material. Moreover, the Superior General informed her that she could ask for a transfer to convents in places where the climate is mild. Ignoring these facts, Sister Lucy stated that her request was mercilessly rejected. Regarding the habit, the Show Cause Notice has the following section:

You uploaded a photo of yours in lay dress in [sic] Facebook and tried to justify your action[s] by criticizing the FCC religious habit in your TV channel discussion. According to the information I [have] got, you stated in your media interviews that our religious habit is not suitable to your life. You should remember that when you joined the FCC Congregation [sic] on 24 June 1982, the religious habit of the FCC was the present one. On 22 May 1985, when you made the first profession of your religious vows, then you received this same religious habit, which you knowingly and willingly accepted. Again on 21 May 1991, when you made your perpetual profession, you were wearing the same religious habit. Please remember that your membership in the FCC is contingent upon the observation of the Proper Law of the FCC. When you joined the Congregation, there were other religious congregations which had other types of religious habits. If you wanted to wear 'a simple Indian dress' you could have joined any one of them. I am not saying that there cannot be any change in the religious habit of the FCC. It is possible. But it should be decided through a democratic process in the General Synaxis, which is the highest legislative body of our Congregation. No member of the FCC can change the norm regarding the religious habit according to her whims and fancies. I am informed that you stated in your TV programmes that you were earlier given permission to use secular dress on certain occasions as you were sent to study in Karnataka. But that was a dispensation given to you by your competent authorities. A dispensation is a relaxation of a mere ecclesiastical law in a special case for a just and reasonable cause after taking into account the circumstances of the case and gravity of the law from which the dispensation is sought (cf. CCEO c.1536). At that time also, you were not permitted to take photos and publish them in lay dress. The relevant question here is not whether churidar [sic] is suitable or bad dress. The question here is this: You voluntarily made your religious profession of vows in the FCC Congregation [sic] and not anywhere else. If you are in the FCC Congregation [sic] you are dutybound [sic] to follow the Proper Law of the FCC Congregation [sic] even regarding the religious habit. You cannot justify your behaviour by stating that many priests wear lay dress. The reply to that is this: They are not bound by the Proper Law of the FCC Congregation. [sic] It is up to their competent superiors to permit or punish them. We should presume that they have the needed permission to do so. You should also remember that not all priests are bound by the norm regarding religious habit[s] as all priests are not religious. As I mentioned in the introduction, there are consecrated women who are not bound by the law regarding [the] religious habit, namely, the members of secular institutes [sic] (cf. CCEO cc. 563-569). Just as there are secular priests who are not bound by the law regarding [the] religious habit, there are also consecrated women belonging to secular institutes who wear secular dress which is simple and modest.

28. Regarding the allegation that Sister Lucy Kalapura failed to take part in community activities, she again argues that it is a fabricated

allegation. However, the local superior reported, and the Chronicles of convent amply testified that this allegation is based on facts to which community members are the witnesses.

29. Regarding the more serious allegations of the violation of the vow[s] of poverty and obedience and the violation of the proper law regarding enclosure, the defence of Sister Lucy refers to her earlier letters. However, in none of those letters [has] Sister Lucy refuted the allegation that she stopped giving her salary to the Congregation since December 2017. That means this allegation [in relation to the subject] of [her] vow of poverty is proven. Sister Lucy did not even promise that in the future she would be ready to change her mind and would start again to give her salary to the Congregation. That means she continues to live in her obstinate and wilful refusal to be faithful to her vow of poverty. In fact, the Show-Cause Notice issued to her has in detail explained to her why this refusal to hand over her salary is a serious violation. We read thus in the Show-Cause Notice regarding this point:

When you made your first profession of religious vows and thus became a member of the FCC, you promised to faithfully observe the rules of FCC. In fact, your formula of temporary and perpetual profession included the solemn declaration that you 'will observe the vows of chastity, poverty, and obedience according to the life and laws of the Franciscan Clarist Congregation.' Moreover on 28 August 2000, you made a declaration of consent, written in your own handwriting and before two witnesses, which contained the following solemn declaration:

During the time in which my membership remains in the said Congregation, whatever I get as gift or through my effort or through any job as salary, wage, allowance, pension, provident fund, insurance, royalty, honorarium, I or anyone of my family members will not have any ownership right or right to use. The right to ownership of all those things are exclusively with Franciscan Clarist Congregation and they are owned and administered according to the Proper Law of the said Congregation.

Despite the declarations and vows, now you claim that the salary you receive is yours! It is true that the Government gives you the salary. As [a] High School teacher, you are getting a good salary of fifty thousand rupees or more per month after all statutory deductions. The Government gives the teachers [a] good salary so that the teachers can pay for their food and accommodation and can buy whatever is necessary for the needed [sic] updating of their knowledge so that they can become competent teachers and so that they can take care of their family as well. In your case, the FCC is providing you with decent food and accommodation, and the FCC provided you [with] everything for your professional updating and is still willing to do whatever is necessary. Your family is the FCC since your first profession on 22 May 1985. You should not forget that when you came to the FCC as a candidate in [sic] 24 June 1982, you had only passed your pre-degree studies with a mere 56 per cent of marks. Your SSLC result was not better either. Thereafter, it was the FCC which took care of all your needs and paid for all your higher studies, including BSc and BEd. As your marks were not that great, it was not easy for you to get admission to the BSc programme. Only because you belonged to the FCC, you got admission to the degree programme. Likewise, the Congregation had to pay a rather big amount to secure for you a place in the BEd programme at Hassan in Karnataka. So if you calculate the amount of money the FCC spent for you in the initial years of your formation, you will see that the Congregation spent a lot of money for you. Even you [sic] got your present job at Dwaraka not because of your personal merit alone, but because of your identity as a member of the FCC. Of the thirty-seven years that you have lived in the FCC, all your expenses including your food, accommodation, dress, travel, medical and study expenses were met by the same Congregation.

It was the decision of the FCC Congregation [sic] to send you for higher studies and get you appointed in the school on a Government salary. It was a decision taken based on your solemn written pledge that as long as you remain in the FCC, your salary will belong to the FCC Congregation [sic]. It was a decision taken based on your profession of vows in the FCC Congregation [sic] where you took the pledge to abide by the laws of the FCC Congregation. [sic] And now you behave as if you did not make any such promise! It is a grave and culpable violation. You are not giving your salary to your Congregation, but you are still enjoying the fruits of your membership in the FCC Congregation like free food and accommodation. And it is sad to see that you do not see any problem in your behaviour. I should state at this juncture that it is now fifteen months that you are fulfilling your obligation to hand over your salary to the Congregation and that is more than seven lakh fifty thousand rupees!

The income of the FCC Congregation [sic] which has 12A income tax exemption is properly audited and the FCC is bound by the income tax rules of our country. We get income tax exemption because we lead a frugal life and we work for the upliftment of the poor and the downtrodden. I do not think that your present lifestyle and the way you spent money will be acceptable even to the income tax department of our country. A good share of our income is spent on the poor and the needy. At the same time, the Congregation also needs money for the sick sisters' medical care, for the training and formation of the new candidates and young sisters. In our Congregation, there are not many who have government salary. [sic] Some of our sisters are working as nurses in Western countries. They all are contributing their whole salary to the Congregation so that we can continue with our work among the poor and the downtrodden. Suppose, if all of them decide like you to not give their salary to the FCC, how do you think that you will be getting free food and accommodation? It was because your seniors who were doing salaried work that the FCC could teach you BSc and BEd. Please do not forget that. If you do not give your salary to the FCC while you continue as a member of the FCC, you are in a way, stealing the money of the FCC, and you are misappropriating the money meant for the poor. I heard that you stated in the TV channel discussions that the FCC has crores of rupees. It is a misleading statement, I should say. If the property value of each community, which is a juridic person, is calculated cumulatively, it is true. But juridic persons are perpetual by nature (cf. CCEO c.927) and their property cannot be misappropriated by individual physical persons. As you know well, our life is simple and frugal and now your life is perhaps the only exception to this. The property of the FCC is neither private property of the Superior General or of the Provincial Superior. It is not the private property of any physical person. It is not public property either. Public property means property that belongs to the Government. It is the property of a juridic person which is recognised as such by the law of the land and are governed by the Property Law of that juridic person under the relevant property laws of India.

It is sad to note that even after such detailed explanation, Sister Lucy Kalapura showed no sign of remorse nor readiness to correct her behaviour in this regard. Hence it is to be considered that Sister Lucy continues in her violation of the vow of poverty on [sic] a grave matter.

30. In her defence letters, nowhere [has] Sister Lucy Kalapura denied that she bought a car in her own name. Likewise she did not produce the required legal permission to buy it. Instead, she justified the purchase of the vehicle as a necessity for her to visit the families of her students in the school. In fact, the Show Cause Notice explained in detail why St. Mary's Province, decided not to have vehicles. The relevant part is given below:

Dear Sister Lucy, you asked permission to buy a car on 28 May 2018 and your competent authority did not grant you the needed [sic] permission. Then also, in clear disobedience, you bought a car in your own name. You should know that though there are seven thousand and thirty-four sisters FCC sisters [sic], [but] you are the only one who owns a private car. Not even the Superior General of the FCC owns a private car. Of course, some provinces and institutions of FCC have got car [sic] in the name of the institutions which are juridic persons. But the Mananthavady Province of the FCC decided not to have any car. This decision was taken by the Provincial Synaxis in order to identify with the poor and to be faithful to the spirit and letter of the FCC Proper Law. *The Way of Life* stipulates in Art. 25 [that] 'our standard of living should be [akin to] that of an ordinary man.' As you know, your province is spread over the District of Wayanad in Kerala, which is one of the poorest districts in Kerala and some neighbouring districts in the nearby Tamil Nadu and Karnataka. There are thousands of poor people in the territory of that province who do not even have the possibility of having enough to satiate their hunger. And there are thousands of families without a decent shelter in the area of your province. In such a context, through the [sic] democratic and collective decision-making process, the Provincial Synaxis of your province decided that the Mananthavady Province of the FCC will not have the luxury of a car, either for collective use or individual use. It was a bold step in the right direction. A car may not be a luxury in some other contexts. But in the context of the poverty of the Wayanad District of Kerala, a religious congregation of the Franciscan family in which the members have taken a vow of poverty, to have a car is a luxury and a counter witness, and in fact, a scandal. Evidently, it is not 'the standard of living of an ordinary man' of the district of Wayanad. It is strange to see that you present yourself as a social worker and a reformer and you live such a life! It is good to ask the question what percentage of the population of the district of Wayanad, who have not taken the vow of poverty, drive a personal car. Do you want to identify yourself with the 10 per cent or less of the rich of your territory, or with the poor? I hereby demand a proper explanation for your action.

It is to be noted that such a detailed explanation of the reasons, why the permission had to be denied to her to buy a car, could not elicit any remorse in her, at least, to apologize for her violation of the vow of poverty. It shows that Sister Lucy failed to understand the real meaning and spirit of the vow of poverty to be observed by a [sic] religious and proves that this is a grave reason which demands her dismissal from the FCC.

31. Regarding the allegation that she published a book without the needed [sic] permission and by spending around fifty thousand rupees too, Sister Lucy did not offer any evidence that she got the needed [sic] permission from her competent superiors. Likewise, she never offered an apology regarding this violation of the vow[s] of poverty and obedience. The Show Cause Notice has the following paragraph regarding this point:

Dear Sister Lucy, on 25 November 2017, you requested permission to publish a collection of your poems. Your Provincial denied the requested permission and suggested that you publish them in *Vachanamrutam* and *Snehadeepthi*. From your file, I see that you were asked by your Provincial to send her the hard copy of the manuscript so that she could assess its quality and worth through some experts; you did not give her a copy of your manuscript. In February 2018, you published those poems as a book entitled *Snehamazhayil* and informed us that it costed [sic] fifty thousand rupees [to get it printed]. If those poems were such a fine work, you could have explored the possibility of publishing them in [sic] Kerala Sahithya Academy or by other publishers who publish works without taking money and even offering royalty. But, instead, ignoring the denial from your Provincial, you decided to spend fifty thousand rupees for publishing it. If you were really concerned about the poor and the needy, you would have realized that it was a big amount of money which could have helped a couple of poor families to survive for a couple of months. Anyway, apparently this unauthorized spending of money is a clear violation of vows of poverty and obedience.

Here too, since Sister Lucy failed to show evidence for the permission to publish the book by spending such an amount; so it is to be concluded that she published it unlawfully. Since she did not offer any apology in this regard, it is to be concluded that she is beyond correction in this regard.

32. The Show Cause Notice formally accused Sister Lucy Kalapura of wilful and repeated acts of disobedience from [sic] her part. The three allegations under this section were the following: 1. Sister Lucy disobeyed the order of the Superior General to meet her in person. 2. Sister Lucy Kalapura did not obey the transfer order given to her in 2015 and that, despite the clear prohibition given in writing to [sic] learn driving and buy a vehicle, she learned driving and bought a car. In none of her defence briefs Sister Lucy denied these allegations convincingly. Regarding the refusal of Sister Lucy Kalapura to appear before the Superior General, the Show Cause Notice has the following paragraph:

On 1 January 2019, through my letter referred to above, I formally asked you in my capacity as the Superior General of the FCC to appear before me on 9 January 2019. On 8 January 2019, you replied me through e-mail that you would not be coming on 9 January as there would be a national strike on that day.

I accepted your reasoning, notwithstanding the possibility for you to travel on the previous day and reach the Generalate on 8 January itself, and on 10 January again I wrote to you asking you to meet on any day between 11–14 January 2019 and to inform me about the time of your arrival. However, you did not reply to that letter of mine. Hence on 18 January 2019, I wrote to you again (cf. Prot. 12/2019). In your reply to that letter, written on 1 February 2019, you argued that your non-appearance before me was not wilful. Let me quote you: 'My non-appearance before you was not wilful. I was not in the mental and physical conditions to travel a long distance.' Dear Sister Lucy, while you claim that your mental and physical conditions prevented you from travelling to the FCC Generalate in Ashokapuram which is near to the Aluva town, it is evident that you travelled to Trivandrum [sic] to participate in the TV channel discussions! According to the Google Map, [sic] the distance from your convent to the Generalate is around 245 kilometres, and it may take around seven hours' car journey. But Trivandrum [sic] is 467 kilometres away from your convent, and it takes more than 12 hours' journey by car. And indeed the way to Trivandrum [sic] passes through Aluva. Hence, I should assume that you obstinately and wilfully disobeyed my legitimate order to meet me in person. It is to be observed that you did not ask for an alternative [sic] date in this regard. Hence your reply given on 1 February 2019 in this regard is rejected as not satisfactory. It is true that you requested for an appointment to meet me in your letter dated 1 March 2019. But from your letter itself it is clear that your request for meeting was to hear you personally regarding your request to wear [a salwar–kameez. This is evident from the following sentence in your letter: 'I will produce the doctor's certificate at the time of the personal hearing.' In my reply dated 4 March 2019 to your letter, I clearly informed you that I would be happy to listen to you regarding your health problem and that I need a copy of the certificate of the doctor.

33. Regarding the allegation that Sister Lucy Kalapura kept a lay person in her room overnight too, she has no apology to offer. From her reply it appears that for her it is not at all a violation of the law regarding enclosure. While she claimed that the person in question was her relative, from an article published by that journalist in *IE Malayalam*, on 15 January 2019, it emerged that she [had] met that person for the first time in her life. Regarding this allegation, the Show Cause Notice has the following paragraph:
According to the proper law of the FCC, not even another sister is permitted to enter the bedroom of one sister of the FCC (Constitutions, 59). However, you have violated this rule by taking a lay person to your room and keeping that person in your room during [sic] a whole night. I consider it as a grave and culpable violation. According to the information I got, that person was not even your blood relative, though *Madhyamam* newspaper reported on 25 January 2019 that the person who spent a night in your room was your relative. If there were [sic] any special urgency to accommodate someone who visited you, you could have asked the local superior and she would have accommodated your guest in one of our guest rooms.

Dear Sister Lucy, you come from a family of eleven: your parents and nine children. Imagine if you were at home and each of your siblings would bring to their bedroom someone of their liking without the permission of your parents, to spend the night together; how would your parents feel? Will your mother appreciate that? I don't think so. If it is so in ordinary families, how much more is expected of a religious (a *sanyasini*) who renounced [sic] the world and took the vow of obedience.

In fact, this Show Cause Notice contains a factual error. Sister Lucy comes from a family of thirteen and not eleven, because she has ten siblings. Otherwise, the Show Cause Notice makes ample effort to elicit at least an apology from her and promise not to repeat such an action in the future. However, Sister Lucy fails to prove that she had the needed [sic] permission to permit that person to stay overnight in her room and hence it is to be concluded that she is in [sic] obstinate and wilful disregard for the Proper Law of the FCC regarding enclosure. Moreover such an act made other members of the convent to live in constant fear as they do not know whom she will be bringing into the convent the next time during night. This is a very grave situation and [a] violation which cannot be simply ignored.

34. The refusal to [sic] Sister Lucy Kalapura to enter the Generalate without being accompanied by a lady officer shows a [sic] totally unacceptable attitude and character of Sister Lucy Kalapura. Her constant criticism of religious life and her suggestion that priests should be [sic] permitted to marry sisters added more confusion and scandal in the minds of many believers and non-believers. Her failure to address the enumerated allegations and her attempt to bring in non-related issues in her defence proved that she is not suited to continue her life in the FCC.

35. Sister Lucy Kalapura failed to show that she had necessary permission to appear before [sic] TV channel programmes. Regarding this, the Show Cause Notice has the following paragraph:
Despite the clear directive from the Syro-Malabar Synod that no religious shall participate in TV channel programmes or shows, without the permission of the major superior, you participated in TV programmes without any permission whatsoever from your competent authority, even after 18 January 2019. Evidence no. 1: According to data available in [sic] YouTube, on 30 January 2019, you appeared in [sic] the TV channel *24 News* for their programme *Janakiyakodathi*. Evidence no. 2: Likewise, *Asianet*

TV channel published [sic] your programme on 30 January 2019 in their programme called *Point Blank*. Evidence no. 3: NDTV published [sic] on 18 February 2019 your interview with them. Evidence no. 4: MediaOne TV published [sic] on 10 February 2019 another interview of yours.

Since Sister Lucy failed to produce any permission from her lawful superiors regarding her participation in the TV talk shows and similar programmes, it is to be concluded that she wilfully and obstinately violated the norm in this regard. Since she did not tender any apology in this regard. It is to be concluded that the two canonical warnings and the Show Cause Notice could bring about the needed [sic] reforms or repentance in her.

36. **Whereas it is proven with moral certainty that Sister Lucy Kalapura FCC violated repeatedly the vows of poverty and obedience which she professed in the Franciscan Clarist Congregation in addition to the Proper Law of the FCC regarding the religious habits and enclosure, and whereas she violated the norm of the Syro-Malabar Church regarding the appearance of religious in TV shows, and whereas both canonical warnings and the additional Show Cause Notice did not bring about the needed repentance or change in her, I, Sister Ann Joseph FCC, the Superior General of the FCC, together with the members of my General Council, hereby dismiss Sister Lucy Kalapura FCC from the same Congregation.**
37. This resolution to dismiss Sister Lucy Kalapura FCC was taken unanimously in the General Council meeting held at Portiuncula, FCC Generalate, Aluva, Kerala, India on 11 May 2019, in which the following members of the General Council were present:

   1. Sister Ann Joseph FCC (Superior General)
   2. Sister Filby FCC

3. Sister Lisa Martin FCC
4. Sister Starly FCC
5. Sister Tresa Jose FCC
6. Sister Betsy Adapur FCC
7. Sister Shephy Davis FCC

38. The decree will be effective only when he it gets the formal approval of the Congregation for the Oriental Churches in Vatican. Once it is approved by the said dicastery, it will be intimated to Sister Lucy Kalapura FCC as early as possible. Against this decree Sister Lucy Kalapura has the right to make recourse to the same Congregation for the Oriental Churches according to the norms of Canon Law. Such a recourse has suspensive effect. If Sister Lucy Kalapura does not propose recourse against this decree within the peremptory time limit set by the law, this decree will become effective and Sister Lucy Kalapura must leave her convent after having handed over her religious habit to her local superior. Thereafter Lucy Kalapura is forbidden by law to use the prefix Sister and the suffix FCC. Since she is entitled to a decent monthly salary, and since she has not handed over to the FCC her salary since December 2017, she is not entitled to any additional financial help on humanitarian ground[s] from the FCC.

Given from the FCC Generalate, Aluva, Kerala, India, on 11 May 2019.

-sd	-sd
Sister Ann Joseph FCC	Sister Filby, Notary/Secretary to the General Council
[stamp]	[stamp]

An Open Letter to the Congregation

It was the duty of the FCC to participate in the fight for justice by the six sisters of Missionaries of Jesus following the continued sexual abuse of one of the sisters by Bishop Franco (Rule N. 80). However, FCC maintained complete silence. God had selected Sister Lucy Kalapura FCC for this mission. Acknowledging and recognizing the same and, till the conclusion of the legal action, supporting and encouraging the six sisters alienated by the Missionaries of Jesus congregation—that should be our mission.

It is not understood why publication of the book *Snehamazhayil* was not permitted even after a long three-year wait (*The Way of Life of FCC14*, 165), (the *Rule and Constitution of FCC N. 86*). You who contend that the *Constitution and The Way of Life*, written in 1973, should be followed unchanged even after centuries that man is more important than laws. Also, recall how in the thirteenth century St. Francis Assisi showed mercy to the brother by his side far beyond what was stipulated. The foundation of all Christian laws is the Gospel. Without that, the religious laws, which go by the letter, will outdo even the civil laws.

How many rules and laws laid down in the *Constitution and The Way of Life* are being followed in the FCC convents? With my experience of thirty-three years in the various convents of Mananthavady Province, I am ready to reveal that the answer is very few.

I, therefore, appeal to you that the unreasonable, gratuitous and continued harassment and mental torture that I am put through by the FCC Mananthavady Province (from 2003) and the Generalate, Aluva may be brought to an end. Is the vow of poverty only applicable to those in Mananthavady Province? All other provinces of the Congregation have many institutions, vehicles and funds and therefore vocations. Have the Congregation's authorities considered why Mananthavady is in such a sorry state that it is not in a position to start and run even a children's nursery properly? If not, they should. After having celebrated monasticism by living in happy spirituality and remaining unperturbed by any adversity, I must live my life in an uplifting manner. I came into the monastery as a free spirit, of my own will, and to live for the community's poor, friendless and those who are denied justice, and thus enjoy my religiosity. I aspire with all my heart to live an even more elevated life in FCC, using all my God-given talent and creativity to this end. I have done and continue to do only such activities as prescribed in the *Constitution and The Way of Life,* though you have alleged that they are violations.

I feel ashamed that the Catholic Church that claims to have a centuries-old heritage is unable to stir itself to action in the case of the nun who was sexually abused thirteen times by Jalandhar's Bishop Franco and is now in a piteous state, being physically, mentally and spiritually down and should receive support and succour. I feel pity for the FCC hierarchy which did not allow me to convey the truth that Nature is Gospel (Rule 60) through my collection of poems titled *Snehamazhayil.* I have a humble request to the Congregation authorities that when they had denied me a car—when I had applied for one (Rule 81) to visit the homes of the poor students whom I teach and to engage with them in a socially responsive manner—they should not have forgotten the Government salary and other benefits they have been receiving over the years. I see an attempt on the part of the Congregation to wear me down and even to obliterate my name. Therefore, the FCC is now a community that denies nuns the rights and considerations that are available any citizen of this country and criticizes a religious life lived as per the Gospel (Matthew 12: 1–8, 11–14, 5: 20; Markose 15: 1–15; Luke 12: 4–7). Once upon a time, Lissy Vadakkel was the Congregation's premier resource for retreats. She was the spiritual leader of many religious groups. Now what has happened? It is now a regime for which right and wrong keep shifting places. I have to say with extreme regret that the Congregation is making grave errors. It should stop hurting Sister Lissy. Please be on the side of truth till at least justice wins.

I am taking another step now with the same determination and fervidity with which I took the first step to become a nun in 1982. For the rest of my life, I have readied myself to live as Sister Lucy Kalapura, to live a genuine monastic life in true spirituality, to mercilessly spurn sham spirituality, and to be the voice of those who have been denied justice and silenced in the Church and society.

Sister Lucy Kalapura
-sd
8 March 2019
(Some passages have been redacted since I have taken names in those.)

References and Further Reading

- 'Bishop Franco Mulakkal and Kerala nun rape case: The story till now', *The Hindu*, 15 October 2018, https://www.thehindu.com/news/national/kerala/bishop-mulakkal-sex-scandal-the-story-till-now/article25227024.ece.
- Maria Abi-Habib and Suhasini Raj, 'Nun's Rape Case Against a Bishop Shakes a Catholic Bastion in India', *New York Times*, 9 February 2019, https://www.nytimes.com/2019/02/09/world/asia/nun-rape-india-bishop.html.
- 'Police should have registered another case against Bishop Franco: Sister Anupama', *Mathrubhumi*, 22 February 2020, https://english.mathrubhumi.com/news/kerala/police-should-have-registered-another-case-against-bishop-franco-sister-anupama-1.4550095.
- Chitleen K. Sethi, 'Why Bishop Franco Mulakkal is among the most powerful Christians in Punjab', *The Print*, 18 October 2018, https://theprint.in/features/why-bishop-franco-mulakkal-is-among-the-most-powerful-christians-in-punjab/136632/.
- Aathira Konikkara, 'Unholy Orders: How Franco Mulakkal wields influence and power in the Jalandhar diocese', *Caravan*,

12 February 2019, https://caravanmagazine.in/religion/franco-mulakkal-wields-influence-power-jalandhar-diocese.
- 'Pope Francis defrocks rape convict Kerala priest Robin Vadakkumchery', *New Indian Express*, 1 March 2020, https://www.newindianexpress.com/states/kerala/2020/mar/01/pope-francis-defrocks-rape-convict-kerala-priest-robin-vadakkumchery-2110663.html.
- 'Rape of minor: former Kerala priest gets 20-year rigorous imprisonment', *The Hindu*, 16 February 2019, https://www.thehindu.com/news/national/kerala/rape-of-minor-former-priest-gets-20-year-ri/article26293358.ece.
- Tim Sullivan, 'Nuns in India tell AP of enduring abuse in Catholic Church', *AP News*, 3 January 2019, https://apnews.com/article/the-reckoning-india-ap-top-news-international-news-asia-pacific-93806f1783f34ea4b8e9c32ed59cdc06.
- Tim Sullivan, 'Long History of Nuns Abused by Priests Unearthed in Kerala', The Quint, 2 January 2019, https://www.thequint.com/news/india/long-history-of-nuns-abused-by-priests-unearthed-in-kerala.
- 'India's hidden years of nuns sexually abused by priests', *Al Jazeera*, 2 January 2019, https://www.aljazeera.com/news/2019/1/2/indias-hidden-years-of-nuns-sexually-abused-by-priests.
- Erik Oritz, 'Pope apologizes for priest sex abuse scandal with "sorrow and shame"', *NBC News*, 20 August 2018, https://www.nbcnews.com/news/pope-francis/pope-francis-apologizes-catholic-priest-sex-abuse-scandal-sorrow-shame-n902121.
- 'Pope admits clerical abuse of nuns including sexual slavery', *BBC*, 6 February 2019, https://www.bbc.com/news/world-europe-47134033.
- Saji Thomas, 'Nuns seek action against Indian priest who fathered a child with nun', 18 December 2020, https://www.ucanews.com/

news/nuns-seek-action-against-indian-priest-who-fathered-a-child-with-nun/90734.

- 'Sister Jesme's book Stuns Kerala Church', *Mumbai Mirror*, 23 February 2009, https://mumbaimirror.indiatimes.com/mumbai-life/sister-jesmes-book-stuns-kerala-church/articleshow/15900392.cms.
- Nidhi Suresh, 'Power, lust and church: Mulakkal verdict brings focus back on sex abuse in convents despite "checks"', *News Laundry*, 19 January 2022, https://www.newslaundry.com/2022/01/19/power-lust-and-church-mulakkal-verdict-brings-focus-back-on-sex-abuse-in-convents-despite-checks.
- Vandana Menon, 'Father, son and the Kerala court — Bishop Franco is free, nuns now in a silent "fortress"', *The Print*, 13 February 2022, https://theprint.in/india/father-son-kerala-court-bishop-franco-is-free-nuns-in-a-silent-fortress/823850/.
- M.R. Subramani, 'Church Ignored Complaints For 22 Years Against Kerala Priest, and This Is How the Serial Sex Offender Was Finally Nailed', *Swarajya*, 20 February 2020, https://swarajyamag.com/politics/church-ignored-complaints-for-22-years-against-kerala-priest-and-this-is-how-the-serial-sex-offender-was-finally-nailed.
- 'Kottiyoor rape: Fr Therakam, two nuns surrender, let off on bail', *The Times of India*, 18 March 2017, https://timesofindia.indiatimes.com/city/kozhikode/kottiyoor-rape-fr-therakam-two-nuns-surrender-let-off-on-bail/articleshow/57699318.cms.

Index

All India Radio, 13
Apostle James, 99
apostolic activities of priests, purpose of, 129
arithmetic, 5
Asianet TV channel, 63

Baby Parunthumplakkal, 115
Bible, 30, 34, 37, 61
Bishop: Franco of Jalandhar Diocese, emergence of, 62, 101, 108, 132; Mar Jose Porunnedom, 108

Carmelites of Mary Immaculate (CMI), 26
Carmelram Theology College, Bangalore, 45
Catholic Church, 86
Chachan, 2–3, 8–9, 11, 14, 18–19, 23, 28–29
cheena bharani practice, 6

Christ Hall, 22
Christians/Christianity, 4, 7, 17, 51
Christmas, 34–35
Code of Canons, 102
Congregation of St. Therese (CST Brothers), 25, 29, 31
Consecrated Life course, 90
convent superiors, 94–95
copra, 15

Deepika newspaper, 62
Dharmaram Vidya Kshetram (DVK), 26
District Education Officer (DEO), 55, 80–83

Eliyamma *chechi*, 8
enslavement, 104
equanimity, 1
evangelism strategies, used by Church, 88

Family Apostolate, 33
farmland, 4
Father: Benny Peekkunnelm, 78;
    George Moolayil, 33; James
    Kannanthanam, 43, 90; Mathew
    Kattady, 72–74; Noble Thomas,
    137–138; Paul Thelekkat, 64;
    Robin Vadakkumchery, 84;
    Thomas Joseph Therakam, 137
Franciscan Clarist Congregation
    (FCC), 16, 24, 39, 41, 50, 60, 73,
    87–88, 97
Franciscan Clarist Sisters, 22
Franciscan order, 123

Gandhi, Rajiv, 26

Holy Communion (first), 116
Holy Mass, 106

Jacob, Ripvan, 78, 85
Jesus Christ, 11, 14–17, 34, 65, 104;
    bride of, 20–21, 87–88
Jose, Jaicy, 42
Joseph, Molly, 75–78, 80
Joseph, P.J., 73

Kalapurakkals family, 4
Karikkottakary village, 4, 10, 23, 28
Kerala Education Act & Rules, 81
kindi, 5
Kota, 28, 31
Kottakkal, Vicar Stephen, 109
Kunjaanjaa, 2, 5, 7–8, 13, 28, 117
Kuppadithara, 32
Kuravilangad, 4
Kurishumala, 107

Kurumbala, 32

Malaparamba, 23
Mananthavady, 23, 25–27, 29, 31,
    34, 113
Mananthavady Eparchy, 72
Mananthavady Provincial House,
    90, 92, 94
meditation, 104
migrants: purchase of land by, 4
migration: due to famine, 4
monasticism, 17, 124
Mother Superior, 15, 18, 23, 28–29,
    31, 34, 106, 130; Ligi Maria,
    108–111
Mother Theresa, 121
mundu, 5
Muthukathani, Regi, 49

New Delhi, 28
Nirmalagiri College, 117
Norbert House, Kuzhinilam, 72
Norbertine Centre, 72
Norbertine Congregation of
    Thalappuzha, 72, 75, 77
nun(s), 2–3, 32, 61, 63, 82, 89, 132,
    136; adopt new names, 123; carry
    tales to parishioners' homes,
    44; change in dress of, 101–102;
    character, 123–124; compelled
    to surrender themselves, 124;
    human emotions, 122–123;
    immorality, 129; public
    declaration of commitment and
    intention, 20; relationships of,
    126; and role of habit, 102; Save
    Our Sister campaign by, 101;

sexual desires of, 126; sexual exploitation of, 127, 129; social life of, 86–87, 104–105; special confession sessions, 127

obedience in Church, 123

paan, 5
Parent-Teacher Association (PTA) meeting, 81
parish priest, 50, 58, 87
Pastoral Centre of the Eparchy, 33
Pastoral Council, 83
Prarthana Bhavan (prayer house), Dwaraka, 103
priesthood, 17, 102
priests, 13, 17, 27–28, 30–31, 33, 35, 44, 48, 50, 57, 72, 75–76, 82, 86–87, 89, 94, 96–97, 102, 105, 108–110, 115, 118, 126–134, 136–137, 139–140; Benny Peekkunnel, 78; homosexual, 128; Subeesh, 77; Thomas, Sunil, 79–80; Vattukunnel, Isaac (Sunil), 58
Provincial Superior, 22–25, 29, 39–42, 83, 87, 90, 92–93, 97

Rosa, 9

Sacred Heart Higher Secondary School, Dwaraka, 31–32, 49, 72, 89
Scaria, Kalapurakkal, 5
Secondary School Leaving Certificate or SSLC), Kaniyaram School, 84

sex maniacs, 128
Sister: Carmaly, 61, 68; Celine Vazhackal, 95; Elamma, 116–117; Elsa, 74; Jemma, 36; Jyothi Maria, 100, 110–111; Lissy, 61; Pavana, 56; Philcy, 51, 96; Rani Maria: (murder of, 29); Rose Francy, 41–42; Sinclare, 43, 73–74; Stephina, 53, 100; Vinaya, 102–103; Vincy, 42
Sister Lucy Kalapura, xi–xiii, 32–35, 62–69, 122, 139–140; appeal for financial help from authorities, 70–71; appointed as: (Mother Superior of Alphonsa Balabhavan, 36–42; personal assistant to Provincial Superior of Assisi Bhavan, 22–23); attended First Holy Communion, 116; complaints on wrongdoings, 80–81; deputed at St. Joseph's Higher Secondary School, Kallody, 54–56; as deputy examination superintendent, 84–85; desire to publish CD of poems, hymns and prose works, 90–92, 100; formations at: (Franciscan Clarist Congregation's St. Mary's Kunnoth convent, 19; Thamarassery Diocese's Franciscan Clarist Convent, Koodathai, 16); and Goa priest manager, 27; joined as English-medium school in Udaipur Diocese, Bhilwara, 47–48; joined St. Mary's

Driving School, 92; mother illness, 96; Mother Superior order to serve as a teacher, 113–114; Portiuncula FCC Generalate in Aluva, training at, 24–26; postulancy year, 17–18; Provincial Superior suggestion for reconciliation, 83–84; pursued: (BEd course in Hasan, 26–27; undergraduate course in Nirmalagiri College, 23–24); removal from Catechism classes and other activities, 109–112; return to Mananthavady, 49–53; schooling and college life of, 10–16; sexual harassment/molestation of, 131–135; training in Bangalore, 43–46; and visit of Provincial Superior to Kommayad convent, 57–61; and visit of journalist friend, 106–107

Snehamazhayil (In Showers of Love), 92

social service, concept of, 11, 13

spirituality, 20, 59, 104

St. Francis Convent, Dwaraka, 32–33

Surajgarh (Rajasthan), 29–30

Syro-Malabar Church, 62, 129

Syro-Malabar Youth Movement/Kerala Catholic Youth Movement, Dwaraka, 33, 64

television, 62

Thalassery province, 23–24, 42

Thoomkuzhy, Mar Jacob, 72

torthu, 5

Vadakkumchery, Robin: sexual exploitation of an underage girl by and relationship with other nuns, 136–137

Vianney Bhavan, 33, 137

virgin land, 4

vocation promoters, 88

Wayanad district, 31, 49, 72

Women's Wall, organized by Kerala government, 101

Youth Ministry, 33

Zion Charismatic Retreat Centre, 33

About the Author

Born to the late Kalapurakkal Scaria and Rosa in Karikkottakary in Kannur district of Kerala, **Sister Lucy** did her schooling from St. Thomas School in Karikkottakary and then went on to study in Nirmalagiri College, Koothuparamba. She joined the convent in June 1982. She took her temporary vows in May 1985.

About the Translator

Nandakumar K. started his career as a sub-editor at the *Financial Express* after obtaining a master's degree in economics. Following a career in international marketing and general management, which has taken him to about fifty countries around the world, he now works for a shipping line in Dubai. He is an empanelled copyeditor and works with Indian publishers and IIM Ahmedabad. He has translated the works of M. Mukundan (*Delhi: A Soliloquy*, which won the JCB Prize for Literature in 2022), the autobiography of Prof. T.J. Joseph (*A Thousand Cuts*) and Indu Menon's short story collection (*The Lesbian Cow and Other Stories*). Nandakumar is the grandson of Mahakavi Vallathol Narayana Menon.